Permission to Break

Permission to Break

A Memoir of Strength, Silence, and Softness

Rashida Saunders

BLACK
EMBER
PRESS

Black Ember Press
Portland, Oregon
www.blackemberpress.com

This is a work of nonfiction based on the author's personal experiences.
Some names and identifying details have been changed to protect the privacy
of individuals. This book also contains references to suicide and mental health
resources. Readers are encouraged to use discretion and seek support as needed.
For crisis support, see Resources (p. 211).

Library of Congress Control Number: 2025920841

ISBN (Paperback): 979-8-9990681-0-1
ISBN (Hardcover): 979-8-9990681-1-8
ISBN (eBook): 979-8-9990681-2-5

Printed in the United States of America
First Edition: 2025

Cover Design: Euan Monaghan
Interior Design: Iram Allam
Photography (Front Cover): Phillyrocket
Photography (Back Cover): Omolola Adeniran

For information or bulk orders,
please contact: info@blackemberpress.com

For Kenzie

You are my greatest reason—my constant
reminder of why love and softness matter.
Every word in these pages carries a piece of you.

Author's Note

The experiences in these pages are drawn from my own life. To protect privacy, some names and details have been changed. These reflections are my own and do not represent the views of any law enforcement agency or organization I have been part of.

This is not a manual or a guide. It is a story—my story—told as truthfully as I know how. What you'll find here is complicated and human: survival and silence, strength and softness, grief and joy.

Some of these pages touch on difficult truths such as trauma, grief, abuse, discrimination, incarceration, and moments of violence. They are told with honesty and tenderness, but they may stir grief, anger, or memories of your own. If you need to pause, please do. If you need to set the book aside and return later, that is okay.

I share these stories with the hope that somewhere in these words, you might feel less alone—and reminded that healing is rarely neat, often nonlinear, and always deeply human. Your care for yourself matters here as much as the story itself.

Contents

PROLOGUE

Woven

Before I ever learned silence, I was already loved. Before I ever became strong, I was already whole. The world taught me to stitch myself together—tighten the threads, hide the frays, and call it survival. But I was never meant to be stitched. I was woven—by God, by lineage, by the women who came before me, by the breath that never left even when I forgot how to exhale. Woven things are imperfect and alive. They loosen. They stretch. They hold. This book is about what happens when the threads finally give way— when silence splits, when survival softens, when we remember that breaking is not the end of becoming. You were never meant to be perfect. You were meant to be free.

PART I
The Weight of Survival

The rules we followed, the silences we learned,
the survival skills we carried long before we
understood their cost.

We learned early how to hold it together.
Silence meant safety. Fighting proved
we mattered. Perfection kept the world
from looking too closely.

These were the tools passed down to us,
sharpened within us, and carried like armor
long—before we understood how heavy
they truly were.

CHAPTER 1

The Courage to Begin

*The ache of living split between
two worlds I carried*

SILENCE WAS THE FIRST LANGUAGE I learned. The hum of the refrigerator filled the kitchen, louder than our conversations ever were. My legs swung against the chair, the scrape of wood on linoleum echoing in a room where no one said what they really felt. I wanted to ask, Are we okay? Do you see me? But I already understood questions had consequences. One sharp glance from my mother across the table was enough to freeze the words in my throat. So I chewed quietly, swallowed them whole, and called it strength. Every word I buried settled in me like a coal pressed under weight, glowing quietly, waiting for a crack.

I didn't know it then, but I was being stitched by survival—tight, careful, afraid to come undone. It would take years to learn I was never meant to be stitched. I was woven—by God, by lineage, by love that outlasts silence.

My mother reinforced the lesson without ever naming it. She stood on the porch most evenings, cigarette balanced between two fingers, smoke curling like a crown above her head. Bills pressed in on the counter. Heartbreak lingered somewhere close by. And still, she never cried in front of us. Once, when tears welled in my eyes after a hard day at school, she said flatly, "Dry it up. Nobody wants to hear all that." It wasn't cruelty. It was survival. Her silence became scripture, and I copied it line for line, not yet knowing that the sacred wasn't in her stillness—it was in the parts of us that longed to be seen.

Softness lived in her too, flickering through the cracks: the night she sang along to the radio, wooden spoon tapping the side of the pot; the time a joke slipped past her defenses and her laughter startled even herself. Those small moments were proof that even in our house of silence, another world existed—one where tenderness was possible.

I learned early that softness was fleeting. So I wore strength like protection. In her silence, I learned the script of one world—hard edges without softness—but somewhere inside I longed for another.

At school, I wore the mask well. Teachers called me resilient. Neighbors said I was strong. After a fight on the playground, my teacher told the class, "Shida's tough. She doesn't let anything shake her." She didn't see my hands trembling under the desk afterward. Resilience was their word for a child carrying too much. Strength was the name they gave to silence. Those compliments pinned me in place—a girl expected to survive without complaint, to straddle worlds, the quiet ache inside me and the tough exterior everyone seemed to admire. I lived in two versions of myself: the girl everyone praised for being tough and the one who carried a quiet, burning ache no one could see.

The armor followed me into adulthood—into motherhood, where tenderness tested what I thought I knew about strength, and into law enforcement, where control became a requirement. My daughter would sit between my knees, her braids clinking with colorful beads as I parted and smoothed each section, her small head tilting back to look at me with a patience that unraveled me. She asked for softness I wasn't sure how to give. In uniform I belonged to one world—steady, composed, unbreakable. At home I was supposed to belong to another—warm, open, present.

Even my hands told the story, caught between light and shadow, belonging to two worlds at once. Family and force. Tenderness and toughness. Black woman and badge. I was living both and—not either or—belonging everywhere and nowhere all at once. I had built a life on this balancing act, but the split was beginning to ache. How long can a person live split down the middle before something gives? One night on patrol made that question impossible to ignore.

"Shots fired," the radio snapped, and the car surged forward. Sirens cut the night open. Streetlights strobed across the dash, painting my hands in alternating bands of shadow and light. My heart thudded so hard I could feel it in my teeth. We arrived to chaos—blood slick on the pavement, voices colliding in fear, someone crying out in grief so raw it hollowed the air. I kept my voice even, my steps steady, my face unreadable. That was the job: unshakable no matter what. But later, long after the scene cleared, my body stayed locked. Heart racing, muscles coiled, breath shallow.

The uniform came off, but the armor stayed. Even in the quiet, my body didn't know the difference between safety and survival. I thought this was strength. What I didn't see was that I was already cracking.

The danger wasn't in breaking. The danger was in pretending I couldn't. The cracks showed up in small ways first—my daughter's laugh bubbling up in the back seat, pulling a smile out of me no matter how heavy the day had been. Bike rides with my older brother, the wind rushing against our faces as we cut through the neighborhood, a reminder that freedom could be simple. Late nights on the porch with my sister, practicing dance routines until our feet hurt, laughing so hard we forgot for a moment that life was heavy. Those moments reminded me joy could still find me, even if I didn't know how to hold onto it. And later, a therapist who didn't rush my silence, who waited until I finally spilled the words I had carried for decades.

When I braced for pity, she gave me presence. "You have a story that needs to be told," she said. I laughed, shaking my head. "Who would care about my story? I'm just a cop. A mom. Nobody. Maybe if I had been through something worse, if my trauma was bigger, my losses heavier, my suffering more dramatic—then maybe it would matter. Other people have stories so much harder than mine. Why should mine take up space?"

She leaned back in her chair, letting the silence stretch until my words felt thin. Then she said, "Pain doesn't have a hierarchy. What you carry matters because you carry it. If you keep minimizing it, you'll keep bleeding in places no one can see."

Her words landed like a challenge. I wanted to argue, to insist I hadn't earned the right to tell this story, but part of me knew she was right. I had spent years comparing my wounds to other people's scars, convincing myself mine weren't deep enough to count. But the truth was, silence doesn't measure pain—it only multiplies it.

I began writing in scraps: notes in my phone between shifts, words on the back of receipts, pages scribbled in the quiet after my daughter went to bed. Writing became my way back—a language softer than survival, truer than silence. Every word I wrote felt like a breath I hadn't realized I was holding. In the space between sentences, I started to feel free.

At first, the sentences were jagged. But slowly they softened. On the page, I didn't have to be strong. I could be messy, tender, human. I wasn't writing for an audience. I was writing for the little girl at the kitchen table who had been taught to stay quiet, and for the woman who had worn two worlds for too long.

Silence was my inheritance, but it was also my suffocation. Strength carried me, but it kept me alone. Survival kept me alive, but it was never meant to be home. I had learned to build a life from endurance, to hold myself together through the ache, to smile and call it gratitude. But there comes a point when even strength begins to crack under its own weight—when the body remembers what the mind tried to forget, when the heart starts whispering for something gentler, something true.

Every story, no matter its shape or size, carries the power to split something open—a wound, a truth, a beginning. And sometimes that split is the only way the light gets in.

It begins in a house where silence was law. It winds through streets where danger and duty lived side by side. It carries the weight of two worlds: family and force, tenderness and toughness, Black woman and badge. That silence shaped me, carried me, nearly destroyed me. This is the story of what happened when silence finally began to open—and I found the ember still burning beneath it.

CHAPTER 2

The Armor We Inherited

*The strength wrapped in silence,
survival passed down as love*

THE GROCERY STORE WAS WHERE I first learned how silence could weigh more than words. Back then, I was small enough to be sent on grown-up errands, pedaling my bike to Safeway with a pre-signed check folded in my pocket—the paper soft from being handled too many times. I clutched it the whole ride, my palms damp, the edges curling under my grip. The bike rattled across cracked sidewalks, my legs pumping not from excitement, but from the knot in my stomach.

Inside, the air smelled of fried chicken from the deli and disinfectant from freshly mopped floors. I rehearsed my smile as I trailed behind the cart, loading basics into the basket. Bread, milk, eggs. Each item beeped across the scanner like a countdown. *Please, God. Please let it go through this time.*

The words left my lips like smoke, rising but going nowhere. I didn't know whether God cared about bounced checks or kids standing in grocery lines with knots in their stomachs. I didn't know if He saw me at all. All I knew was that my prayer hung in the air like the pause at the register, unanswered and suspended in silence.

The total climbed higher; my chest tightening. The cashier, a woman with tired eyes and a name tag that read Shirley, barely looked at me as I slid the check across the counter. The register paused, a beat too long, and my ears roared in the silence.

Then the letters appeared: NSF. Non-Sufficient Funds. I didn't know what those letters meant, but I understood the look, the sigh from the cashier, the impatient shift of the person behind me, and the heat rushing up my neck. NSF didn't feel like a bank code; it felt like a verdict. Not enough money, not enough help, not enough me.

She handed me the slip, flimsy and merciless. No bags, no food, nothing to carry home. I walked out empty-handed, but the absence weighed more than anything I could have held. I climbed back onto my bike; the paper crumpled in my fist and pedaled toward home. Each push felt heavier, as if the hollowness itself pressed down on me. The wind slapped my face, sharp and cold, but I did not cry. I pressed my lips together the way I always did when tears threatened—tight enough to keep them in, tight enough to keep myself from unraveling. That was the day I stopped feeling like a child.

Scarcity has a way of erasing innocence before you are ready. I remember another day, not long before that one, when silence cut just as deeply. It was my birthday. No balloons, no cake, no one marking that it mattered. The TV buzzed in the background, dinner smells drifted from the kitchen, and the hours ticked by without acknowledgment. I told myself it was fine, that birthdays were for other kids. Lying in bed that night, I felt the ache settle in, the confirmation that I was not someone worth celebrating. That belief followed me, shaping the way I reached, or didn't reach, for love.

There were nights without food, mornings when the water was shut off, and days when the electricity flickered out. In my neighborhood, that was not unusual. Struggle was not the exception, it was the air we breathed. I didn't envy kids with new shoes or cable TV. I envied the kids who were given permission to cry. The ones with dads at pickup and moms who kissed them just because. Kids who could pout, whine, or fall apart without being told to toughen up.

I didn't want things, I wanted tenderness. I wanted someone to notice when I was quiet and ask if I was okay. Affection was not the language we spoke at home. No hugs waiting at the door, no casual I love you. I didn't even realize what was missing until it appeared in flashes.

When I was four or five, my mom rubbed circles on my back while I lay sick in bed. Her hand moved steady and soft until I fell asleep. For that night, I felt seen. Years later, on the bus ride back to school after a field trip, my head slumped against my first-grade teacher's shoulder. She slipped her arm around me, and though the touch startled me awake, I kept my eyes closed just to hold it a little longer. I hadn't craved touch until I felt it; then I could not forget it.

Occasionally, my mom gave us flashes of joy too. She tickled us until we couldn't breathe, her hands quick and relentless, her laughter spilling out like something she rarely let the world hear. We collapsed in a pile, gasping for air, my sides aching, tears running down my face from laughing too hard. In those minutes, the whole house exhaled with us.

It never lasted. The laughter always dissolved into quiet, as if joy were a guest we weren't supposed to let stay. I learned to carry both truths at once: my mom loved me, and her love came in pieces—rationed and fleeting. I taught myself to savor joy quietly, because asking for more felt like asking for too much. Better to take what was given than risk being told it was all I would get. That is how you learn to ration love, not because you want to, but because you are afraid of needing too much.

The Armor We Inherited

The absence of harm is not the same as the presence of love. A house without yelling can still feel cold. A childhood without bruises can still be one without affection. Just because no one raised their voice doesn't mean you were heard, and just because no one raised a hand doesn't mean you were held. Safety and love are not the same. Safety keeps you alive, love reminds you why living matters.

The world thinks children are resilient. I know now that what we call resilience is often just silence in disguise. It is a child hiding her tears, so no one calls her weak. It is swallowing needs, so you won't be disappointed when they go unmet. It is carrying pain quietly because you have learned that naming it will not change anything. That is not resilience. That is survival. And survival leaves scars.

Silence became my first defense. I can't remember the exact moment I learned it. Maybe it was during one of my mom's arguments with my stepdad—or at school when a teacher once made a joke at my expense. I remember the heaviness of my tongue, the way thoughts pressed against my teeth and never came out. I told myself it was safer not to speak. If I didn't argue, I couldn't be wrong. If I didn't ask, I couldn't be disappointed. Silence kept me out of the line of fire, but it also built walls around me.

Years later, I wrote a letter. Wide-ruled paper, purple gel pen, folded into neat squares and tucked under my pillow until I was brave enough to hand it over. Dad, can we go to the park? Will you play basketball with me? I waited. Days, then weeks. Each afternoon I ran to the door at the clatter of the mail slot. Envelopes scattered across the rug. My heart leapt, then sank when not one carried his name. Maybe tomorrow. Maybe he forgot. Maybe he was busy. Nothing came.

His silence wasn't loud, but it was absolute. That was the day I swallowed a new belief: if I didn't ask, I couldn't be disappointed.

It was easier to quiet myself than to risk another unanswered letter, easier to believe my needs were too much than to face the truth that he would not come. The paper became proof that my voice was safer folded away than spoken out loud. Silence didn't just hide me, it rehearsed me for a life of vanishing in plain sight.

At our dinner table, silence had manners. Forks clicked, the TV hummed in the next room, and the clock over the stove kept counting even when I wished it would stop. "Are you tired?" I asked my mom once. "Tired is part of life, Shida. You just keep going."

She didn't look at me when she said it. Her hands kept moving, cracking eggs into a pan, flipping toast onto plates. The muscles in her arms flexed with a weariness she never named. I nodded and pushed food around my plate. The words I wanted hovered like steam, then cooled back inside me. Please ask me if I am okay. Please tell me I matter. Please say you love me. My throat burned, and I swallowed it down. That's how it worked, the body learned to hold what the world would not.

Black daughters are taught this early. We learn to swallow what might make us look needy, fragile, or ungrateful. We learn that softness can be used against us, that silence is safer than being misunderstood. Silence wasn't just survival in my house; it was survival in the world.

I tried once with my mother, writing her a note after she called me a name that stung. She read it, laughed, and repeated it on the phone to a friend in a mocking voice. I never wrote another letter. The first one had gone unanswered, the second became a joke. Together, they taught me the same lesson: my words were safer unsaid.

Even years later, sitting across from my first therapist as a police officer, silence followed me in, stitched into my skin as tightly as the badge I wore. I knew how to look composed, how to sit upright with steady eyes, how to answer with just enough honesty to seem cooperative while keeping the truth buried. I edited my pain into bite-size pieces, served up smiles to soften the edges, and performed "fine" like it was part of the uniform.

Being seen felt dangerous; silence still felt safe. Yet healing does not happen in hiding. Healing demands the risk of unraveling in front of someone else, of speaking the words you've swallowed of trusting that broken does not mean beyond repair.

This is not about blaming our parents, it is about naming what we inherited and choosing what ends with us. They loved us the way they knew, through protection and provision. Honoring that truth doesn't mean repeating it, it means choosing something softer. *Armor can keep you alive, but it cannot help you live.* Survival is not freedom, and endurance is not the same as joy.

At some point, we deserve more than just breathing through the days. We were never meant to be impenetrable. We were made to be human—to feel without apology, to risk closeness, to let love reach us. To be held not because we earn it, but because we exist.

So if you were raised in silence, this is for you. I know how it teaches you to carry everything alone, as if your body were the only container strong enough to hold what no one else will touch. I know how it convinces you that protecting your pain is safer than speaking it. But you do not have to carry that weight anymore. You do not have to guard the wounds that fractured you, or protect what already broke you.

We get to learn that love does not require silence to survive. I am still learning to speak, too. Silence shaped me, but it also sharpened me. But here is the truth I had to dig out of my own throat: silence didn't just hide me—it rewrote me.

Silence taught me how to fold myself small, how to disappear without ever leaving the room. But it also taught me to listen for the parts of me that refused to stay hidden.

I'm learning that love does not require silence to survive. I am still learning to speak too. It taught me how to endure, how to keep moving when I wanted to collapse. Here is the truth I had to dig out of my own throat: silence didn't just hide me, it rewrote me. It turned a little girl who only wanted to be loved into a woman who believed love had to be earned through strength, composure, and disappearing parts of herself to make others stay.

The body remembers every unspoken word. Silence does not disappear—it calcifies. But silence was not the only inheritance. There was another lesson I didn't ask for but still received: how to fight. Not always with fists, sometimes with posture, with presence, with the readiness that anticipates danger before it arrives.

I didn't ask for the fight, life gave it to me anyway. And over time it became instinct. What I couldn't see was this: the same silence that erased me also equipped me. It taught me how to be sharp, how to stay watchful, how to hold my ground in a world that wasn't always safe. But the cost was steep. Living in constant defense meant that softness became a stranger, rest felt unsafe, and real love felt like a risk too costly to take.

Still, something in me stirred. A whisper said there is more. What I carried was not only inheritance—it was instruction. The world demanded that I be ready before I was grown, and so I was. Childhood did not wait for me—it pressed me forward, teaching me how to stand my ground, how to protect myself, how to fight.

Silence was the first armor I wore, but it was not the last. In the cracks where quiet could not hold me, fight began to grow. It was rougher, louder, and just as costly, yet it felt like the only way to matter. That was the next lesson I learned: when silence breaks, fight takes its place.

CHAPTER 3

When Silence Taught Me to Fight

The battles my fists carried
when words could not

THE WEAPONS SURVIVAL GAVE ME, and the ache of never putting them down. I never set out to be a fighter. Life, raw and unpredictable, didn't leave me with another choice. By the time I was ten, I had learned that survival required more than silence or words. It required my body—both as shield and as weapon.

One day stands out. The bell rang and the hallway spilled into laughter—sneakers squeaking, cheap bracelets clattering like secrets no one dared to say out loud. Outside, my backpack straps dug into my shoulders, each step heavy with books and homework thumping against my spine. I should have been thinking about snacks or cartoons. Instead, I was listening for footsteps. Behind me, as always, came the teasing.

"Why you talk like that?"

"Think you better than us?"

"Ugly. Stuck-up."

Sometimes I pretended not to hear. Sometimes I walked faster. But words travel; they know how to find you. That day, the shadows caught up. She stepped in front of me, chin tipped high, blocking the sidewalk like a door I was not allowed to open. "Say something now." Her hands shot out and shoved me hard in the chest. It was not just the shove. It was the message: *You don't belong here. You don't get to walk away.*

Something in me snapped. My backpack hit the ground with a dull thud. Sneakers screeched against pavement. My fists moved before my mind did, wild and desperate. I tasted blood where I had bitten my lip. Around us, kids shouted, voices rising into a frantic roar.

Inside, a quieter voice begged, please don't make me do this again. I swung anyway. No adults came. No one stepped in. This was how kids without safety handled conflict, with fists, fear, and fury. When it was over, I stumbled home buzzing with adrenaline. My chest throbbed. My knuckles ached. My stomach churned with shame. Underneath it all was something I did not yet have words for: pride.

At home, my mother stood at the stove. She did not scold me. She did not hug me either. She looked at me with eyes dulled by exhaustion and said, "Sometimes people will try you. Make sure they never try you twice." That was it. No lecture. No comfort. Just law, laid down like concrete. And I received it like gospel. Her words were not only hers. They were an inheritance.

Black mothers have long known the world would come for their daughters early, and softness would not protect us. They taught us to harden, not because they did not want us to laugh or play, but because innocence is a luxury we are rarely allowed to keep. I did not know it then, but that moment in the kitchen was bigger than a single fight. It was initiation into a lineage, girls trained to defend themselves before they were ever allowed to simply be children. That was my first fight. It would not be my last.

By middle school, the fighter in me was not new; it was expected. My name carried weight in hallways, not for grades or sports, but because people knew I would not back down. "If you mess with her, you better be ready," I overheard once. The words landed like a crown and a curse. I did not go looking for trouble, but trouble found me. A sideways look on the bus. A rumor whispered too loud. The wrong joke. One girl snatched my binder; before I knew it, I had her pinned against a locker, rage ringing in my ears louder than the crowd chanting, "Fight! Fight!"

The truth was, I hated it. After every fight my stomach knotted, and my hands trembled long after the crowd dispersed. In my neighborhood, fear had to stay hidden. Pride had to be louder than shame. Vulnerability was a luxury we could not afford. I wore the reputation instead, pretending it fit better than it did. Still, I wondered what it might feel like to be just a kid, laughing in the bleachers, walking home without scanning for threats, saying "sorry" instead of throwing punches. I longed for the ease of softness, but no one taught me there could be another way.

I remember one night after a fight, walking home alone. Sweat clung to my shirt, drying sticky on my skin. In the bathroom mirror, I caught a face I barely recognized—hair wild, lip split, eyes glassy with adrenaline. I wanted to cry, but the tears would not come. Even with no one watching, I could not let myself soften.

The streets had rules. Do not let anyone punk you. Do not show weakness. Do not cry where anyone can see. Respect was not given; it was fought for—earned with posture, presence, and sometimes blood. I kept my chin high. I learned to read people the way some kids read books, quickly, carefully, searching for the ending before it arrived. I was not the biggest or the loudest, but I was sharp, watchful, and ready. Readiness, practiced long enough, hardens into identity.

"Fighter" was not just what I did; it became who I was. I was not only fighting with fists. I was fighting the silence I had been taught to keep. Sometimes holding my tongue hurt worse than bruised knuckles. Strength was not simply modeled in my house; it lived in the air we breathed. It was stitched into our bodies before we even had language for it. You did not cry, you did not break, you did not stop moving.

I remember my friend Samantha teaching me this without ever meaning to. She came over most mornings, walking with me to the corner store first, then to the bus stop. It was our ritual. One morning, as soon as she stepped through the door, our dog lunged toward her. Before I could grab him, she bolted. She sprinted across the street without looking, scaled an eight-foot fence topped with barbed wire, and vanished in seconds.

By the time I caught up and calmed her down, blood was dripping from her hand where the barbed wire had ripped it open. The cut was wide and deep. I felt sick, but Samantha pressed her palm against the wound, shrugged, and walked on as if it were nothing. No tears. No complaints. That day, she showed me the rule we already knew: Black girls did not cry. Even in fear. Even in pain. You walked it off. Not long after, I learned the same lesson in my own body.

I was riding my bike down Fifteenth toward my aunt's house near Fremont, flying down the hill, every sidewalk crack caused my tires to rattle beneath me. I felt myself losing control, slammed on the brakes, and in the next moment I was airborne. For a split second it felt like freedom, everything still and weightless, then the pavement rushed up and knocked the breath out of me. I skidded belly-first, skin tearing across both elbows, my stomach, my wrist, and my palm.

I froze, dazed, until I heard the rumble of a TriMet bus behind me. Pride shot through me like lightning. I jumped to my feet, forcing myself to stand straight until the bus passed. No one could see me broken. Not here. Not now. When I tried to lift my bike, the handlebars were twisted backward. Out of frustration, I left it and limped the rest of the way to my aunt's. Every step burned under the summer sun, raw skin stinging with each movement. What I wanted was my mom—someone to notice, to say, Shida, that looks painful. I knew better. That was not an option. I did not cry. I soldiered on.

Between Samantha's barbed-wire hand and my own body scraped raw against concrete, the message was clear. Pain was something you carried, not something you showed. To cry was to lose. To pause was to fall behind. Strength was not in the healing; it was in the hiding. I learned to fight in ways that had nothing to do with fists, against weakness, against fear, against the part of me that wanted comfort.

Survival was its own kind of battle, and silence was the sharpest weapon I had. I did not know how well that training would serve me—or how deeply it would wound me. The lessons I learned on cracked sidewalks and under buzzing streetlights followed me into adulthood, slipping under my badge, into my relationships, into the way I carried grief. They taught me how to keep moving, but not how to stop. They gave me armor, but not a way to take it off.

That was the pivot I could not yet name; the girl who fought to be unbroken was becoming the woman who struggled to lay her armor down. By the time the academy tested me, life already had. In a scenario-based training exercise, I was cast as the "civilian." My instructions were simple: approach the officer in training and lightly poke him in the chest. I stepped forward, calm and steady, protective gear strapped tight. The mat smelled like rubber and old sweat. Before I could reach him, my feet left the ground.

He launched me. The world flipped. I hit the mat so hard the air shot out of me. My ears rang. My body screamed. For a moment, all I could hear was the thunder of my own heartbeat. The instructor crouched beside me. "Who's the president? What year is it? Where are you?" I answered just enough to pass, then pulled composure over my pain like a mask. Class ended. I drove home in silence, every pothole vibrating through my ribs. The ache was not just physical. It settled low and heavy, an old knowing humming beneath the bruises.

Out in the real world, there are no mats, no whistles, no instructors ready to call time. If you are slammed to the ground, there may be no one to ask if you are okay. No report. No accountability. Just impact—and silence. Then came the question I could not outrun: if I had not been in uniform, if I had just been another Black girl in my neighborhood, would anyone have stopped? I already knew the answer.

That day was not only training. It was recognition. I was not just a police recruit. I was a Black woman thrown to the ground without cause, reminded what it feels like to be on the receiving end of power wielded too quickly. It was not lost on me that I was one of only a handful of women in that room, and the only Black woman. Toughness was demanded of me in double measure, but softness would be read as weakness. If the men were proving strength, I was proving survival, proof I could take the hit and still stand, proof I belonged. No one named the cost of carrying twice the weight in a room that already measured me differently.

Power without empathy is dangerous. Training without accountability is dangerous. Surviving without reflection is another kind of harm. That moment did not make me bitter. It made me intentional. It clarified why I was there. I had not come to law enforcement to perform power. I came to protect, to become the presence I once needed, to choose compassion where others might choose control. Real strength is not in the slam. It is in the pause, the restraint, the choice not to escalate simply because you can.

Over time, I became fluent in confrontation, not only with fists, but with posture, with silence that cut, with eye contact held long enough to tip a balance. The academy gave me tactics; life had already given me instincts. No one tells you the cost. Constant readiness becomes a prison. You do not clock out when your shift ends. You do not relax at the dinner table. In restaurants you sit with your back to the wall. In grocery stores you are already mapping exits. Driving home at night, your heart jumps at every shadow in the rearview mirror. Even joy becomes suspicious. Laughter keeps an edge, as if you are waiting for the turn.

At night my body jerked awake at the smallest sound. My muscles stayed coiled, ready to spring. Sleep was shallow, a place I visited but never truly rested. I called it strength. Most days it felt like exhaustion. Fighting did not only shape how I moved through the streets or trained at the academy—it shaped how I loved. I kept people at arm's length, mistaking distance for safety. I confused control with care. Even in moments that should have been tender, I stayed braced.

Relationships became another arena: Me proving. Me posturing. Me protecting. And underneath it all, what I longed for most was rest. The fighter kept me alive, but she also kept me lonely. It was not only joy I was missing. It was grief. Grief requires openness. It asks you to let the ache rise instead of pinning it down. I had trained myself to hold, to lock everything away. I carried my losses the way I carried my fights—tight in my chest, hidden under composure, wrapped in strength. But grief does not knock. It storms in. When it came for me, I was not ready, not for the silence it left behind, not for the way it whispered, you cannot fight your way out of this one.

I learned to outrun sadness with service. When the feelings swelled, I said yes to more shifts. I volunteered. I checked every box I could find. If I was useful, I did not have to feel. If I was needed, maybe I would not be needy. On paper I looked dependable, reliable under pressure, steady in crisis. Inside, I was bargaining with my own heart. I told myself I would rest later. Later never came.

I wish I could say the fighter only rose when I needed her. Fighting is a habit as much as a response. Sometimes she showed up in conversations that could have been calm. I clenched when I could have listened. I sharpened my voice when I could have asked a question. I built cases instead of building trust. I won arguments and lost closeness. I was safe, but I was not seen.

If you want to understand a fighter, ask about her teachers. I think about my mother at the stove, passing me that concrete law: "Make sure they never try you twice." I think about the women who raised me in rooms where softness had a price—where keeping your guard up kept you breathing. I think about Samantha pressing a bleeding hand against her shirt because missing the bus carried its own consequences. I think about a girl on a bike, standing tall on shredded skin so strangers would not see her break. I think about the recruit who hit the mat and answered every question right just so she could leave the room with her dignity intact.

I honor them all. I thank them. And then, when I can, I let them rest. Now I am learning to fight differently—not to survive, but to protect my peace. Not to prove, but to preserve. Not to harden, but to hold boundaries around my softness. I can set the glove down and still be strong. I can pause and still be safe. I can cry and still be whole. I still carry the fighter inside me. She is sharp. She is brave. She is necessary. She is not all of me. I am more than what I have survived.

Some days I still hear my mother's law—make sure they never try you twice—and I smile. I know what she meant. I also know there are other ways to be untried. You can answer to your own name instead of every dare. You can choose softness that does not surrender, a tenderness that remembers where you have been but refuses to live there. The world will still come for us early. Some doors will still slam.

There is another inheritance I am building—one my daughter can carry without it breaking her back: the right to rest when she is hurting, the right to ask for help, the right to be a child for as long as she is one. The right to grieve without apology. The right to laugh without checking the room first. Fighting was never just about fists, it was about proving I belonged, even when the world told me I didn't.

Childhood taught me how to stand my ground, but it also left me carrying a weight I couldn't name. Growing older didn't take the fight out of me, it only disguised it. The lessons of childhood sharpened into new demands: achieve more, be more, never slip. What began in survival turned into performance, and the higher I climbed, the narrower the path became. I thought fighting meant survival. But what I didn't realize was that the battle wasn't only out there, *it was also inside of me.*

CHAPTER 4

Raised at the Edge of Survival

The childhood shaped where
love and danger lived side by side

I LEARNED EARLY HOW TO BALANCE on a line so thin; it barely existed. On one side was the pull of failure, on the other the demand for perfection. I carried both as if they were the only options. Success was never about joy; it was about survival. Every grade, every smile, every achievement was proof that I could keep moving forward. But beneath the surface, I was exhausted. Childhood had ended too soon, and the world never stopped asking for more. By the time I reached college, I knew how to perform almost anything —except rest.

The blur began in middle school. Chaos was the language, and I was fluent. Hallways slammed with lockers, the air thick with sweat and gossip, sneakers screeching against tile floors. I remember crouching in a backyard with friends, skipping class, passing a blunt between us. The smoke clung to my hoodie, sweet and acrid, staining my clothes in a way no amount of Febreze could hide. We laughed too hard, collapsed onto the grass, and dared each other to keep quiet while neighbors shouted at us to knock it off. We thought we were untouchable—until the day we were not.

Seventh grade nearly cost me everything. By then I was cutting class more than showing up, drifting like a shadow. One afternoon, a teacher caught me slipping out of the building and marched me to the office. I sat across from the principal, arms crossed, face blank, pretending I did not care while my stomach twisted tight. The office smelled of pencil shavings and disinfectant—a sterile kind of cleanliness that made my chest constrict. They slid the paperwork across the desk. Suspension. Maybe expulsion. The bold black letters blurred, pressing down like a verdict already decided. For a moment, I saw the script written for kids like me, and I almost believed it was mine.

In that moment I saw two futures. One swallowed me into the script already written for kids like me. The other asked me to fight like hell and refuse to hand them the pen. The daughter in me— the one who didn't want to add to my mother's burden—snapped into focus. I promised I would pull it together, keep my grades up, and show up in class. Somehow, they believed me. They gave me another chance. That was the line. I could have been another dropout, another statistic. Instead, I walked out carrying a scar no one could see, one I never forgot. Where I came from, survival was the curriculum. Anything beyond that was extra credit.

Survival was not only about grades or discipline. It was about hunger. Imagine being eleven and calling your coach, not for shoes or rides, but for grocery money so your family could eat. I should have been asking for rides to practice, not learning how to ration twenty dollars across four mouths. The phone felt heavy in my hand, slick with sweat as I dialed, my voice catching before the words came out. And to be clear, my mother never told me to ask. I simply knew that if I didn't step up, we would go without.

I used to watch her come home bone-tired, dropping her keys on the counter like they weighed a hundred pounds. Some nights, she pushed food around her plate and insisted she was not hungry, but I knew better. She was making sure there was enough for us. Hunger was not just mine—it was hers. That's the part no one saw —the way mothers swallow their own need so their kids can eat. I mistook that sacrifice for silence until I realized it was love. And here's the truth: love without softness still leaves you hungry.

Then came my stepdad. He arrived like a promise for a while— money where there had been none, groceries filling the fridge, a hand that unclenched my mother's worry just enough to let a tired smile through. When he was around, life breathed easier. We ate. The lights stayed on. For the first time in a long time, I saw my mother rest. It felt like safety, and for a time it was. But safety in our house always came with a shadow. His addiction lived louder than his presence, and safety splintered as quickly as it came.

Safety in our house had a temper. The man who could make the bills vanish could also summon chaos in quieter, corrosive ways. Until the night the police were called. Until I walked into the living room and found him slumped on the couch, eyes glazed, his body sunk deep in a haze no words could reach. The cycle was brutal. He was gone, then back, then gone again. Each return brought a fragile calm that splintered as quickly as it came.

My mother's strength was never in the absence of struggle. It was in her endurance through it. Watching her taught me early that survival itself could be love, feeding us, shielding us, keeping us from falling apart. There was a cost to that kind of love. It taught me to be careful with asking, to measure my needs, to smooth down my edges so we could keep the fragile structure of the household intact. Love became logistics: food, bills, a roof. Tenderness was a rare guest.

Beyond our walls, the neighborhood had its own rhythm. Sirens cut through the night as often as laughter, and cracked sidewalks doubled as basketball courts. Aunties passed out plates of food just in case, while kids ran barefoot between cars. It was love and danger at once. Violence was never far—the crack of gunshots interrupting block parties, murals painted too soon for boys who never made it to twenty.

I remember one night when the shots rang so close that my body hit the floor before my mind caught up. The sound tore through the block, and voices scattered like marbles across concrete. Later, we learned it was a boy from a few streets over, someone's cousin, someone who had been laughing just the week before. Life and death could trade places that quickly, without warning.

I wasn't tempted to join a gang to survive, but my older brother didn't have the same privilege. I remember the slam of the front door when he left and the low voices calling his name down the block. The paths available to boys and girls in our world were different—not because choices did not exist, but because consequences did. Boys shouldered certain risks. Girls shouldered others. The soil was the same—hunger and absence and the ache of not being seen—and from it grew very different survival scripts.

Drugs hollowed out houses, turning neighbors into ghosts, while joblessness pressed down on families already stretched thin. You could feel both the closeness and the sharp edge of survival in the air. The same hands that passed you a plate could also steer you away from a corner after dark. Joy and risk lived side by side, and we learned to hold both without letting either break us.

That blur—the push and pull between danger and joy—shaped the way we moved. Long summer nights on courts, a radio booming. Double-dutch battles until our calves ached. Sneaking through sprinklers fully clothed. Those were the handfuls of joy we clutched. We laughed like we were trying to outrun something. Even then, joy and grief lived in the same body. You learned to carry them both.

I was worn down by the weight of my surroundings, desperate for a way out of the cycle I saw around me. I didn't know exactly what I was reaching for—only that I needed something different, somewhere that might give me permission to change. My mother wanted that too. She hoped a new school might offer more stability, fewer distractions, a chance to start fresh. For me, it wasn't just about opportunity—it was about survival, about finding a place where I didn't have to keep shrinking just to stay safe.

High school felt like stepping onto foreign soil. Walking into my private school, I felt the weight of two worlds pressing against me. It wasn't an elite academy—but it was a step up from public school. The floors gleamed, polished under shoes from stores I had never entered. The kids weren't only well-off—they moved through a different universe. The hallways didn't smell like anything at all— just air, clean and empty, nothing like the fried food and dust that clung to home. They compared summer trips and SAT prep courses, while I folded my free-lunch ticket into the smallest square possible, praying it might vanish between my fingers.

At home, I downplayed it. At school, I performed it. I lived in translation—too much for where I came from, not enough for where I was headed. That translation was its own blur—belonging everywhere and nowhere at once. One afternoon it was sealed. A classmate leaned across the desk and asked where I lived. I hesitated before saying the name of my neighborhood. His eyebrows rose, just slightly, and then he muttered, "Oh… damn." The word wasn't loud, but it cut deep enough to remind me that some people would see a statistic before they ever saw me. In that moment, I realized the wound isn't always the word itself—sometimes it's the reminder that you've already been judged.

Nights told the truth. After practice, I retreated to the room I shared with my younger sister. She was always there—her quiet breathing, the soft rustle of blankets, the steady rhythm of her presence. Books lay scattered across my bed; my planner crammed with assignments I could barely keep up with. My body was worn thin, and in those late hours, between her quiet and my exhaustion, the weight pressed hardest. Laughter floated from other rooms. Inside mine there was only stillness. I could ace the test, win the race, get the grade—and no one would know how heavy it was to carry two versions of me at once. The world saw achievement. I felt absence. That was the blur—looking successful on the outside while silence hummed like static inside me.

Sometimes the blur showed up in my body. I remember sitting in class, everything quiet and normal, when suddenly my chest tightened, and my heart raced. The clock ticked too loudly. Nothing had happened, yet my body was bracing like a fight was about to begin. I swallowed it down, kept my face steady, and raised my hand to answer a question as if nothing had shifted inside. That was survival disguised as composure. That was the cost of living— blurred between fighting and becoming.

Excellence didn't quiet the ache. It only covered it, the way paint hides a crack until it spreads. I learned to smile through the sting, to nod instead of snap back. Silence became my safest mask, even when anger rose hot in my chest. And still, there was joy. Joy in late-night phone calls, whispering secrets until the line clicked. Joy when our basketball team won. Joy when our 4x100 relay team took state. Joy in a teacher pulling me aside to say, "You're special. Don't forget it." Joy in bus rides home, singing off-key with teammates, fries greasy with salt passed around like communion. Some nights I fell asleep with cheeks sore from laughing, proof that joy could live in the same body as grief.

By graduation I was not just receiving a diploma. I was shedding a skin, proof that survival isn't the same as becoming. And if you've ever walked across a stage carrying pride in one hand and guilt in the other, you know what I mean. I was proud, and I was guilty. Guilty for leaving my mother to hold everything together without me. Guilty for stepping into a world she had worked so hard to give me access to, even though she had never had it herself. I remember her face that day, half pride and half exhaustion, and I carried both expressions with me. If survival had been her gift, then excellence had to be my repayment.

When I left for college, I had exactly twenty-one dollars to my name. Not enough for books, barely enough for food, and certainly not enough for the kind of induction I thought college kids were supposed to have. If my friend had not offered me a ride with her parents, I do not know how I would have even gotten to campus.

In my mind, I had pictured my mom dropping me off, helping me unpack, maybe even fussing over where to put my things. That was the way it seemed to happen for other kids. But that was not our story. My mom was working, surviving, carrying more than anyone should. My stepdad was in the house, but not the kind of steady presence who would help move boxes into a dorm. His addiction had already shown me the difference between being physically there and being reliable. And my dad, I did not even think of asking him. Silence had already taught me which doors were closed.

I told my mom not to worry, carried my bags into the car with twenty-one dollars in my pocket, and let my friend's parents drive me toward a future I was not sure I could afford. That was my move-in story. No fanfare. No family photos on the steps of the dorm. Just me learning again how to do without, how to stand on the edge, and how to keep moving forward.

College felt like breathing new air. Independence. Possibility. A chance to figure out who I was outside survival. I carried it all with me: the high-functioning student, the silence I had learned to live with, the grief I never named. On the surface I was thriving. Inside, I was crumbling in ways no transcript could show. There were nights when the laughter faded. After the pizza boxes were emptied, the music cut, and the door closed, I lay in bed staring at the ceiling, silence pressing in like a weight. Even in a crowded dorm I could feel alone. Even surrounded I could feel unseen. That was the blur too, being in the room but not in the moment, smiling while part of me stood off to the side, arms crossed, waiting for the crash.

One night in a dorm common room, a friend looked me in the eye and asked, "Are you okay?" No one had ever asked it like that, as if the answer mattered. My throat burned with words I did not know how to say. I laughed it off, but something shifted. Maybe it was possible to be seen without performing. Maybe it was possible to be cared for without earning it. Vulnerability felt dangerous. I was tired of pretending.

There was joy here as well. Joy in blasting music and dancing wild in my dorm until our faces hurt from smiling. Joy in decorating my first room with posters and string lights, claiming a corner of the world as mine. Joy in late-night pizza runs and spontaneous road trips, in voices screaming lyrics into the night sky. Joy in collapsing on dorm room floors after hours of talking, laughter dissolving into comfortable quiet.

College did not save me. It gave me room, room to breathe, room to question, room to begin again. Those years sharpened skills

I would carry into adulthood: how to scan a room before I entered it, how to read people like textbooks, how to live between worlds. But silence was still there, patient as ever. I blurred between survival and becoming, carrying joy in flashes and shadows in silence. I could perform excellence, laugh until my cheeks ached, even taste freedom in small doses. Underneath it all, I was tired. Tired of holding hunger in my body like a secret. Tired of pretending I did not flinch at judgment. Tired of carrying two versions of myself everywhere I went.

College gave me distance, but not relief. I knew how to excel, how to perform, how to keep moving forward as if achievement could erase the ache underneath. From the outside it looked like I was thriving, but inside I was worn thin. I had been trained to keep it together, to smile and succeed, to never let the weight show. That training became a mask. And the mask had only two words: I'm fine. Excellence could hide almost anything, even despair. And that disguise followed me into adulthood.

Still, underneath it all, the truth remained. I was raised on the edge, between hunger and hope, danger and joy, silence and survival. The edge sharpened me, but it also left me tired. Excellence became my camouflage, the way I hid the cracks so no one could see how close I was to breaking. Looking back, I know now I wasn't the only one caught in the blur. So many of us learned to smile while carrying absence, to succeed while starving for softness. The edge is not the only place we belong. Survival may have shaped us, but it is not all we are. What lingers after survival are the scars we can't always see, the ones that live beneath the surface and echo through every silence that follows.

CHAPTER 5

The Scars of Silence

*The marks left by words
we were never allowed to speak*

FUCK. SOMETIMES THAT IS THE ONLY WORD that fits, the only word big enough to hold what silence burned inside me. Anger felt dangerous, so I buried it deep. I clenched my jaw until my teeth ached, balled my fists until my nails carved crescents into my palms, and swallowed the heat rising in my throat until it settled like a stone in my stomach. I thought silence made me safe. Unspoken pain doesn't vanish; it smolders. And sooner or later, it burns.

No one told me faith could hold anger too. I believed rage and prayer could not coexist, so I buried one and performed the other. I clenched my fists in secret and folded my hands in public, as if God only wanted the polished version of me. No one said prayers could sound like shouting, or that God could handle the fire in my chest. I learned to split myself in two, anger tucked into silence, faith pressed into performance.

I learned early on that showing rage could cost you respect, opportunities, even safety. Instead of exploding, I imploded. My body became the container for everything I could not let out. I see myself small again, standing in my grandmother's living room, jaw clenched so tight it ached. An adult had just corrected me, sharp and dismissive, for "talking back." The truth was, I wasn't talking back. I was telling the truth. But in our world, truth could sound like disrespect, and disrespect could earn you a slap. I bit my tongue and swallowed the words that burned in my throat, tears stinging but never falling. On the outside, I looked composed. On the inside, my chest felt like fire.

That was the rule: hold it in. Be quiet. Be "ladylike." Do not let your anger show. As a Black girl, I learned early that being too loud, too honest, or too unfiltered could get me in trouble. I became fluent in silence. I smiled when I wanted to scream. I laughed when I wanted to cry. I stayed composed even when I was breaking. Silence does not erase what you bury; it ferments. What I pressed down did not disappear. It grew heavier, sharper, and hotter until the weight of it seeped through the cracks. Rage doesn't die when you ignore it. It waits. It simmers. Eventually, it demands a voice.

Fuck. Fuck this. Fuck him. Fuck her. If you know me, you know I enjoy cursing, not always because I am angry, but because I can. Because I wasn't allowed to. I grew up in a world where you had to hold it together. Being "ladylike" meant being quiet. Expressing emotion was seen as weak, dramatic, or disrespectful. I stayed in line. I played the part. I learned to be composed, even when I was crumbling inside.

I learned early what it meant to swallow fire and pretend it wasn't burning. My mother's voice was sharp as a slap, her words landing before I could get mine out. I don't remember exactly what I said. Maybe it was a protest. Maybe it was the truth. I remember the heat rising so fast it scared me. My fists clenched at my sides. My jaw locked. My heart pounded in my ears. I wanted to yell. I wanted to throw something, break something, prove I wasn't made of stone.

Instead, I swallowed it. Her eyes dared me to speak again. I knew the rules. You do not talk back. You do not raise your voice. You do not show her you are angry, even if you are right. Especially if you are right. I bit my tongue until it hurt, pressed my nails into my palms until half-moons rose on my skin, and said nothing.

Silence wasn't only my rule. It was our inheritance. My mother swallowed her rage too. My grandmother did before her. In our family, pain was carried quietly, passed down like heirlooms. We did not cry in public. We did not raise our voices. We endured. It was survival, and I wore it like a second skin. Anger wasn't only about how it felt inside me. It was about how dangerous it looked to other people. A girl's anger was "disrespectful." A Black girl's anger was "too much." And mine, in that kitchen, was a fire with nowhere to go.

I learned the rules in every room. At home, anger had permission to exist—just not mine. My mother could slam a door and let the fire fly. My brother could rage, storm out, and come back when the air cooled. But me? My job was to stay quiet. To listen. To absorb what no one else wanted to hold. At school, speaking up made me "defiant." On the block, mouthing off could turn into a fight. Later, when I wore a uniform, anger became a trap. The badge gave me authority but demanded control. Too much fire and I wasn't "professional." I was a problem.

I trained myself to keep my voice even, my face unreadable, and my body still, even when inside I was burning. Silence does not just bury anger. It buries grief. The academy calls it composure. They teach us to steady our voices, to walk into the worst day of someone else's life and make order out of the wreckage. Clear the scene. Take a statement. Carry the pain of strangers like evidence, and pretend to leave it at the end of the shift. They taught me how to do the job. They did not teach me what to do when the uniform felt too thin

35

to hold what I carried. They did not prepare me for the moments when protocol could not protect me, when the silence after a call was louder than the call itself, when the badge felt too small for the weight I bore.

What startled me wasn't that I cried. It was where. At work. In uniform. In front of everyone. The tears arrived uninvited and unstoppable, not the discreet kind you can wipe away, but the kind that crash through all your composure. My throat burned. My vision blurred. I felt exposed and embarrassed. I also felt human. In a profession where emotions are treated like liabilities, that kind of humanity feels dangerous. Silence always has a price.

My jaw ached from clenching through too many "yes, ma'ams" and "I'm fine." I woke with fists balled in my sleep, nails pressed so deep into my palms they left marks. My stomach knotted before hard conversations. My temples throbbed after long days of pretending everything was okay. My body learned silence before I had words for it. Every clenched jaw, every sleepless night, every nail pressed into my palms was muscle memory passed down, proof of what generations before me had carried and never spoken. Sometimes the fire leaked out sideways.

One night, someone I loved brushed past a boundary like it was nothing. A joke that cut too deep, a touch that ignored the pause in my body, a laugh that told me my feelings were too much. My chest tightened, heat rising fast. I wanted to scream, to tell them how much it mattered, to let the truth fly. Instead, I crossed my arms, swallowed the words, and pulled away. On the inside I was raging. Later, when the silence stretched between us, I realized that swallowing my fire had not protected me—it had isolated me. That's what silence does—it convinces you you're keeping the peace when really you're cutting yourself off from it.

There was one night I almost let silence take me all the way under. I sat in my car after a shift, smell from my uniform still clinging to me, radio off, headlights cutting through the dark. I had held it together through another call, another family's worst day, another night of pretending I was fine. The second I closed the door, the quiet was deafening. It pressed against me, thick and heavy, until it felt like I couldn't breathe. My jaw ached. My fists pulsed. Underneath the rage was something even scarier: nothing. A hollow so deep I wondered if disappearing would finally bring relief. I thought about how easy it would be to not show up tomorrow, to let the silence swallow me whole.

The scariest part wasn't that I thought it. It was how calm it felt, how ordinary the thought sounded in my head. That was the moment I realized silence wasn't just muting me. It was erasing me. If I did not find a way to break it, it would break me. That is when the room appeared. A couch. A clock. A box of tissues I refused to touch. My legs crossed. My hands folded in my lap like I was in church, still and guarded, holding myself together like a prayer I wasn't ready to speak. The hum of the air conditioner sounded too loud in the stillness.

"Why are you here?" she asked.

I wanted to spill everything: the grief I had buried, the exhaustion I wore like a second skin, the fire I had swallowed since I was ten, standing in the kitchen. But instead, I reached for the safest truth I could manage.

"I'm just tired," I whispered.

She slid a yellow legal pad across the table. "Write the thought that won't leave you alone," she said. I lowered my pen and wrote: *I am too much.*

She drew two columns. Evidence for. Evidence against. "Let's put that sentence on trial," she said, and handed me the pen. My palm sweated. The rule had survived a lifetime of silence. It did not survive the page. Another day, she placed two small buzzers in my hands. "Hold the picture," she said, moving her fingers left then right. The disks hummed, a rhythm I could feel more than hear. The kitchen. The dare in my mother's eyes. The heat rising up my neck. The hum kept time until the scene loosened its grip. The memory did not vanish. It released me enough to breathe inside it.

We practiced words I had never learned. Not big speeches. Simple sentences that made room for me. "When you interrupt me, I feel invisible because I need respect. Will you let me finish?" The first time I said it, my voice shook. The second time, it did not. I took those sentences into my life like new shoes I was afraid to scuff. At dinner, a loved one reached for my plate before I was done. Old rage ticked on like a metronome. I set my fork down. "When you take my food before I'm finished, I feel dismissed. I need choice. Would you ask me next time?" Her hand froze. Mine did not.

With my daughter, the mirror was even clearer. She stomped her foot and shouted. My instinct was to hush her and make her small. I caught myself. I crouched to her level. "You are angry. That makes sense. You wanted a say. I want that for you too. Let's try again." I watched her face soften. I felt something in me soften too.

Little by little, I learned that what I had called strength was often just survival. Crying in uniform was not weakness. It was a breakthrough. Anger was not my enemy. Silence was. Therapy did not fix me. It freed me. It showed me that silence had never protected me. It had imprisoned me. The more I spoke, the more I lived. For so long, I thought the fire beneath my silence would burn me alive. Now I see it for what it was: proof that I was still here. Proof that even in the quiet, my spirit refused to be extinguished.

I am no longer afraid of my anger. I trust it now. It does not make me dangerous. It makes me whole. I am no longer bound by silence. Speaking does not make me weak. It makes me free. Healing was never about holding it in. Healing was always about telling the truth.

The silence I carried was not only mine. It belonged to generations. Every time I speak, every time I let my fire burn without shame, every time I name what grief has done to me, I do more than free myself. I break the chain. I think back to that night in the car, headlights cutting through the dark, when silence almost convinced me I did not matter. Then I think about now, about how I speak, how I rage, how I cry, how I love. Silence did not win. I did.

And if the first word I ever claimed for my rage was fuck, then let the last word I claim for my freedom be the same. Fuck silence. Fuck the lie that I was ever meant to disappear. The silence that burned had one final lesson. When you learn to speak, your work does not end. You only change the fight. Finding my voice was just the beginning. The truest test came when I put on the badge, when strength was expected to speak louder than pain, and silence became part of the uniform. But silence never stays contained. It seeps into everything, even the way we learn to carry strength.

PART II

The Weight of the Badge

The armor I wore, the cracks it could not hide

The badge gave me a language the world
respected, but it also deepened the silence
already stitched deep within me.

Armor followed me into every call,
every room, every night at home. What
I carried beneath the uniform never
stayed hidden for long.

CHAPTER 6

What the Fire Couldn't Take

*The dignity that endured when
everything else was burned away*

THE BADGE LOOKED LIKE ARMOR, but it couldn't carry what I carried inside. It couldn't hold the grief that clung to me after every call—or the silence I brought home at the end of each shift. On the outside, the uniform signaled strength. On the inside, it magnified every fracture I had been trying to hide. Motherhood had opened me to tenderness, fear, and a longing for honesty. The badge demanded that I shut it all down. In one world, I was someone's safe place; in the other, I was expected to be impenetrable. The collision between the two nearly crushed me.

Policing rarely felt like work when I was in my flow—shooting hoops with kids in the park, photobombing prom pictures, letting joy lead in ways the academy never prepared me for. Those moments weren't scripted; they happened because kids trusted me enough to let me in. One afternoon at a local community center, the music kicked on and a line dance broke out. I was in uniform, firearm on my hip, but the kids waved me in like I was one of them. I jumped into the line, boots shuffling across the gym floor, laughter spilling out as we moved in sync. The room roared with cheers, and for a few minutes the badge didn't matter, just rhythm, sweat, and joy.

Another time, before a Trail Blazers game, I was standing in the main lobby when the Blazer Dancers came out to hype up the crowd. *Walk It Out* blasted through the speakers, and without thinking, I jumped in, matching their moves. The energy was electric—wild and uncontained. Fans circled around, phones shot into the air—and the lobby erupted in cheers. I laughed until my sides ached, dancing so hard, that sweat gathered under my vest.

It was messy, loud, unplanned—and just as necessary for me as it was for them. For a moment, the badge disappeared into the background. What remained was connection: wild, imperfect, and exactly what we all needed. But even in that freedom, the badge was never far. It waited in the silence after the music stopped, in the stares I caught from parents who weren't sure what to make of me, in the knowledge that joy could vanish the moment the radio crackled with another call. My mother's dignity had taught me to stand tall, to meet the world without shrinking. But that same dignity also meant she never fully trusted the uniform I chose.

To her, the badge was just another face of power, and power had never shown up gently for us. To me, it was a chance to prove otherwise: to make service look like something different. Basketball in the park. Reading to kids. Dancing until the whole gym shook. I wore the badge hoping to carry her lessons and undo her suspicions at once, even if that meant holding two truths that never quite touched: her survival and my service, her suspicion and my hope. And in between them, I tried to carve out moments like that line dance or lobby dance, fleeting proof that joy could still break through, even under the weight of the shield.

I didn't learn dignity in a classroom or the academy. I learned it from my mom—on hot pavement, cigarette smoke curling above her head, refusing to shrink even when she was in the wrong. The memory is burned into me: Safeway on MLK, groceries scattered after an officer said he had to tow the car. Milk sweating onto the pavement. My mom lit a cigarette like it was her last word. She didn't plead. She didn't apologize. She didn't let her shoulders bend under the embarrassment. She stood tall, smoke rising like a crown, while I balanced heavy bags and tried not to cry.

People in our neighborhood whispered that cops were dangerous, untrustworthy. I heard the warnings in barbershops, on porches, in the quiet after sirens faded. Authority was something to fear, not to trust. But at home, I saw something else. I watched my mom stand her ground, curse them out, demand her rights, make them remember her name. She didn't flinch; she didn't fold. Even if she walked away with a ticket or without a car, she never walked away without her dignity.

What I couldn't see then was how much that moment echoed the lessons I had already learned as a child. Silence was my first armor. Composure, my first survival skill. By the time I put on the badge, those tools had simply changed shape. What began as shrinking at the dinner table became standing unflinching on the street. Reading my mother's moods became reading strangers before they spoke. The survival that once kept me safe at home became the same survival I carried into uniform.

Back then, I believed survival meant disappearing, keeping my head down, swallowing words that might draw heat. I thought safety lived in silence. Watching my mom, I learned another way. Her survival wasn't quiet; it was refusal. It was meeting power without surrendering your own—standing tall even when life pressed its weight on your chest. Survival could be fierce. It could be loud. It could be a declaration: I am still here. You will not erase me.

The seed of becoming a cop was planted right there—between an officer's words about a suspended license and the silence that followed. People ask why I chose policing like the answer should be simple. It isn't. I have more than one. I wanted to protect my community, especially the kids who didn't feel safe. I wanted to be the person who showed up when called, because as a child, that mattered. My mom didn't always get consistency from family, but every time she dialed 911, someone came. Maybe, watching them, watching her, I believed authority didn't have to mean intimidation. It could mean presence.

When I pinned the badge to my chest, I carried more than an oath. I carried my mother's fire—her refusal to fold. I carried the silence I was raised in, the kind that taught me to swallow pain and keep moving. I carried the survival skills that trained me to read a room before I walked through the door, to anticipate danger before it arrived, to stand tall even when my insides trembled. And I carried the tiny hand of my daughter, the hand that once reached for my face and reminded me I was human beneath the armor. That hand was my compass, the steady reminder that power without tenderness isn't strength at all.

The truth is, I didn't choose policing because I loved authority. I chose it because I knew what it felt like to be invisible. I wanted to stand in the gap for people who felt unseen. I knew how chaos presses in, how hunger shapes choices, how silence swallows voices. The badge, to me, wasn't just about law; it was about dignity— about meeting unseen weight with compassion, not contempt.

One call still stays with me. Late summer. Heat clung to the air. Dispatch sent me to check on a man pacing outside a corner store, shirt torn, muttering to himself. When I pulled up, I saw the tension in his body, the way people gave him a wide berth. Another officer might've gone straight to commands. I saw the fear in his eyes, the tremor in his hands. I kept my distance. Lowered my voice. "What's your name?" I asked. He didn't answer at first. Then, barely a whisper, he told me. I used his name again, steady, gentle. I told him I wasn't there to make things worse. I asked who he wanted me to call. He said his sister. Ten minutes later, I leaned against my car as she pulled up, tears on her face. He climbed in without a fight. No shouting, no headlines—just dignity: his intact, mine intact.

There were dozens of nights like that, times when presence, patience, and voice mattered more than force. Times when showing up human changed the ending. Times when I remembered why I put the badge on in the first place. Dignity became my quiet resistance—not against the work, but against a culture that mistakes intimidation for authority and silence for strength. Authority, for me, was never about proving who held the power—it was about leaving people with their humanity intact. True authority wasn't measured by how small I could make someone feel, but by how much dignity they still carried when the moment was over.

But dignity came at a cost. It meant standing out when blending in would've been safer. It meant whispers, sideways looks, laughter that wasn't harmless. It meant peeling off the uniform at night and barely recognizing the reflection, eyes harder than I wanted, shoulders tense in stillness, a face older than my years. It meant lying awake, asking if I was changing anything—or just breaking quietly, in slow motion where no one could see.

The cost wasn't only inside the department walls. It was in the streets too. Some in the community saw my badge before they saw me. To them, I wasn't Rashida, I was the uniform, *the weight of history*, the face of every injustice that came before me. Some inside the department saw my softness before they saw my strength. To them, I was too different, too willing to listen, too willing to bend where the culture demanded I harden.

I learned what it is to straddle two worlds and belong to neither. Too "cop" for parts of my community, too "community" for parts of my peers. A loneliness no one prepared me for—the ache of loving two places that didn't fully trust you back.

There were nights I thought about walking away. I'd sit in my car after a shift, radio silent, hands aching from the wheel, chest tight with everything I couldn't name. I'd think about Kenzie asleep at home and, wonder if the job was stripping away the softness she needed from me. She deserved my laughter, my light. Some days, all I had left were the edges.

Then morning feet would patter down the hall. She'd fling herself into my arms before I could set my bag down, laughter spilling like it had been waiting all night for me. She didn't care about the badge or the weight I carried—only that I was hers. In her arms I remembered what dignity was really for. Not just to survive the job. Not just to stand tall against the world. But to make sure she grew up with a mother who could still soften, still laugh, still love without apology. She reminded me humanity wasn't optional, it was the point.

That's the paradox no one teaches: dignity will save your soul, but it won't always save your standing. It keeps you human in places that want you hardened, and it can leave you lonely when you refuse to become what the culture demands. Resistance kept me from disappearing; resistance is heavy when you shoulder it daily.

The badge didn't just test my courage; it tested my humanity. Every shift asked me to carry both, and every shift chipped at the balance. Courage—I knew—I'd practiced it since childhood. Holding on to my humanity, refusing to let the job strip the softness I fought to reclaim, was the real work.

Here's the hidden weight any role can carry: the world asks you to armor up and rarely stops to ask what it costs to live that way. That isn't only the story of policing—it's the story of being human in a world that confuses domination with power, silence with resilience, and survival with strength.

The truth is, we all wear some kind of badge. Some are metal. Some are stitched into job titles, others into family roles. Some are invisible, the mask of *I'm fine*. Whatever form it takes, the badge comes with expectations. Be strong. Don't waver. Don't let them see you sweat. We can live like that for a while, but eventually the weight catches up.

I carried mine in my body. Tightness in my chest, headaches that never released. I carried it into sleep. Sirens wove themselves into dreams and loud sounds snapped me awake. I carried it into motherhood. I stood in my daughter's doorway, wondering if all I had left to give her were the edges. That's the cost no one sees, the quiet erosion that never makes reports or headlines.

Dignity was my shield, and some days, my wound. It kept me human, and some nights, it left me alone. And still, I couldn't set it down. Surrendering my dignity would have meant erasing myself completely, and I had already lived a childhood where silence wrote too much of my story. I refused to let adulthood do the same. I held the line, even when it hurt. I carried courage and humanity, even as they pulled in opposite directions. In the quiet, a question grew: How long can a person live split down the middle like that?

Maybe the invitation isn't to choose between courage and humanity at all. Maybe it's to refuse the lie that they can't coexist. What would it look like to carry both, not flawlessly, not without cost, but honestly? To stand brave without hardening. To stay tender without disappearing. To live not as fragments, but whole—softness and strength, dignity and vulnerability, side by side.

And then, something else: I wasn't always standing alone. People inside and outside the department, saw past the badge. They recognized the human beneath the armor. They reminded me that carrying dignity didn't have to mean carrying it by myself. Brotherhood and sisterhood showed up in unexpected places—sometimes loud and protective, sometimes quiet and steady. In a world that kept asking me to harden, those relationships softened me in ways I didn't know I needed.

I entered policing with my mother's chin high and my child's hand in mine, believing dignity could be a different kind of authority. I still believe it. Joy was never the absence of tension; it was my refusal to let tension decide who I would be. If I had to stand in the middle, I would stand there human, present, unshrinking, leaving people with their dignity intact, including my own.

The badge gave me purpose, but it also built walls. What steadied me were the bonds that formed in the cracks, the quiet sisterhood and brotherhood that caught me when the job let me fall. They became my second family. Some offered laughter that stitched me back together after the hardest nights. Others carried sharp edges—hardening me in ways I never asked for but couldn't escape. Together they became the family I never saw ones who saved me, scarred me, and shaped the version of me that survived.

CHAPTER 7

The Ties That Bound Me

The weight of loyalty I carried
but could not escape

THE WORDS "I GOT YOU" have carried me further than strength alone ever could. I did not always trust them, did not always believe them, but over time they became the thread that bound me to sisterhood and brotherhood, the bonds that held me when I could not hold myself. There's a kind of love that only grows in the middle of chaos—in patrol cars and briefing rooms, in midnight calls and living rooms flooded with blue light. Bonds were forged that defied explanation. We did not choose each other the way friends usually do. The job chose for us, and in those unlikely pairings I found brothers and sisters who held me up when I could no longer carry myself.

Other rooms held me too, the kind with low music and clinking glasses, where perfume gathered like a soft halo and fresh flowers leaned toward the center of every table. Heels tapped out quick rhythms on tile. Laughter rose and fell like waves. A hand brushed mine in passing, light and casual, and my chest tightened anyway. I smiled when eyes met mine, tilted my head in practiced warmth—and braced on the inside.

51

It is a strange ache to stand in the middle of so much brightness and still feel the chill of loneliness press close. To look like you belong while a quieter part of you whispers that you do not. I learned to hold a wine glass steady, to nod at the right stories, to let laughter rise at the right beat, yet the whole time another voice cautioned, do not get too comfortable, this is not yours to keep.

For most of my life, I believed I had to be self-sufficient. Needing anyone felt like failure. Sisterhood sounded lovely in theory, and dangerous in practice. When you're taught to survive, you're rarely taught to trust. I had been conditioned to protect myself, even from other women, especially from them. Competition, betrayal, and comparison—these were the stories I absorbed. We were taught to stand out, not to lean.

Maybe that is why tenderness felt foreign when it finally arrived. I did not grow up watching women fold into one another's arms or lay burdens down where they could be shared. My mother stood alone, fought alone, and carried alone. Strength meant solitude. Softness between women was a language I'd never heard spoken. When it showed up later in my life, I did not recognize its accent. I had to unlearn suspicion, unlearn armor, and practice letting care reach me.

Even before Alpha Kappa Alpha Sorority, Incorporated, there were women, non-Greek friends, who became my first quiet lessons in sisterhood. Three-hour calls that wove laughter and tears into a single thread. Dinner and wine nights where we spoke our dreams into existence. Long city walks that turned into therapy without the title. They held the broken pieces of me, turned them gently in the light, and treated them as precious. I did not always believe I deserved kind of care, yet they offered it anyway. A seed took root. Maybe trust wouldn't undo me.

When I joined Alpha Kappa Alpha, it was not only about sisterhood. It was legacy, service, excellence. It was insisting on high standards while making room for the parts of me I kept hidden. On the night of initiation, my heart pounded beneath the weight of tradition. Pride and fear lived side by side in my chest, pride that I had made it here, that I belonged to something bigger, and fear that one day they would see through me and decide I was not enough.

Membership did not end with ceremony. It unfurled into life. Conferences and boardrooms. Community events on chilly mornings. Late-night calls when someone needed prayer or a plan. My line sisters became my mirror and my compass. They held me accountable when I wanted to hide, asked me to dream out loud when I'd forgotten how, and loved me even when love was the last language I could receive.

They were the ones who turned ordinary nights into medicine —car karaoke sessions with windows down, music blasting, our voices cracking on high notes and laughter spilling into the air. They were the ones who crowded into a small room for my baby shower, wrapping me not just in gifts but in presence. The love was felt in those small moments, the kind that do not make headlines but build foundations. I remember standing at their weddings, watching them walk down aisles lit with joy, my own heart swelling as if their vows stitched themselves into my story too. Sisterhood was not just the public moments. It was private promises whispered in their own ways: I got you.

I didn't always welcome their tenderness. After years of holding myself up, softness felt like a country with rules I did not know. Their presence made me restless, as if love itself pressed too close against wounds I kept bandaged. When they hugged me, my body went rigid—before it remembered how to melt.

One night, they dragged me to a crowded restaurant after a week that had hollowed me out. The room glowed with warmth. I laughed at the jokes, nodded at the stories, and gripped my breath like a handle. Then one of them leaned in and asked, "How are you—really?" The tears came before I could stop them. Not the neat kind, but the kind that breaks through your guard and baptizes you where you sit. Mascara blurred, shoulders curled inward, and my hands shook in my lap.

She reached across the table, pulled me into her arms, and did not let go. Instinct told me to freeze, hold your breath, keep still. She rocked me like the aunties used to rock babies after church, a soft hum low in her throat. My jaw unclenched. My fists softened. A dam ruptured. My arms lifted, clumsy at first, then certain. The sobs rolled out from a place older than I was.

I cried for every time I had swallowed my needs, for every night I convinced myself I was fine, for every room where I confused silence with safety. The tears came heavy, carrying years I hadn't let myself name. She absorbed it all without flinching, her stillness holding what I could not. That night I learned something I had never believed possible: vulnerability does not always strip you bare. Sometimes it stitches you back together. Sometimes it restores you.

I can count on one hand the times my line sisters have seen me cry, not because the tears were not there, but because I had not given myself permission to let them fall. And yet, they never rushed me. They waited. They stayed. They took the time to truly know me beyond the armor, beyond the practiced smile, beyond "I'm fine." Allowing them to see me, really see me, has been one of the most impactful choices of my life. That is what real sisterhood does. It refuses to wait for your polished self. It meets you messy, mascara streaked, shoulders shaking, and holds you tighter.

Not every moment was perfect—some rubbed raw, some healed slow. There were times when differences rubbed against each other, when silence between us felt heavier than words. But even in tension, sisterhood was practice, learning how to stay, how to repair, how to love each other in the middle of our imperfections. What mattered most was not the absence of conflict, but the presence of women who chose to keep showing up anyway. Sisterhood was not only tenderness in private rooms. It was work in public ones.

When I was invited to attend my first Annual Leadership Fellows Program, I knew I was stepping into something remarkable. Designed for selected undergraduates, it offered a space to develop and expand leadership skills both professionally and within Alpha Kappa Alpha. Acceptance into the program was not casual. It was a recognition of women who embodied exceptional leadership, demonstrated academic achievement, and carried a commitment to excellence.

I remember walking into the ballroom, nerves humming under my skin. My blazer felt like both armor and costume, sharp at the shoulders but soft where my palms smoothed it again and again. The air was thick with coffee and fresh linens, and everywhere I looked were women who seemed carved out of brilliance, polished voices, poised shoulders, confidence rolling off them like light. I kept aligning the notepad in front of me, hoping no one could see how small I felt inside.

During one of the opening sessions, we went around the table sharing why we chose Alpha Kappa Alpha. The women before me spoke with ease: about legacy, about mothers and grandmothers who had worn the same letters, about service projects that ignited their purpose. When it was my turn, my throat tightened. For a moment, the silence pressed too heavy, and I thought about shrinking back into it. Then, I caught the eye of a sister across the table.

She nodded once—steady and certain—like she was loaning me her breath.

"My story is different," I said, voice thinner than I wanted. "I didn't grow up with this language of sisterhood. I'm still learning it. But I came, because I want to believe belonging can be real. I came because I want to grow."

The room didn't flinch. Instead, they leaned in. And in their leaning, I felt something shift. By the end of the program, I wasn't just walking taller because I had learned about leadership strategies or career planning; I was walking taller because I had been seen, because these women, brilliant and accomplished, had made space for my voice.

That week taught me that legacy is not a word to be admired, but a responsibility to be carried. It is not only about who came before me, but about how I will make room for those coming after. For the first time, I felt the weight of belonging not just to a chapter or a line, but to a lineage of women who had been preparing spaces like this long before I arrived. And yet, as much as sisterhood was shaping me, brotherhood was teaching me too, though in an entirely different language.

In law enforcement, I was surrounded by men who became like brothers. Some tested me, jabbing at my armor to see if it would clang or crack. Others stood quietly at my shoulder when the temperature dropped after I spoke up. Brotherhood rarely arrived with lilies or long talks. It showed up as presence, a steady look across a room, a nod that said, I see you, without asking for anything back.

Early on, a veteran watched me walk into a briefing where doubt hung like fog. Afterward, he pulled me aside and said, "You do not have to prove yourself to them. Do the work, and let the work talk." It was not tender, but it steadied something in me that had started to shake. That was brotherhood at its best; not flowers, but a hand at the small of your back that keeps you upright when the room tilts.

There was always a moment—the quiet before the noise—when I could feel the weight of what the uniform demanded. Another night, the field turned feral. A narrow street, too many voices, heat rising from the pavement in a wavering veil. The crowd pressed close enough for me to feel the static on my skin. Before panic could take root, I felt a quiet nudge on my shoulder, just enough to say move with me. My partner slid half an inch closer, planted his feet, and said into my ear, low and certain, "I got you." Three words that cut through the noise—my breath slowed, my stance widened. We moved as one. That is what brotherhood did, it lent you its spine when yours threatened to give out.

It was not always clean. Sometimes care arrived as warnings that doubled as walls. "Do not let them play you. Do not show too much. Do not trust too quickly." Those rules kept me safe, and they also thickened my armor on days when I was trying to take it off. Brotherhood kept me from folding, and it made softness harder to practice.

Both came at a cost. Sisterhood stretched me into vulnerability before I felt ready, its persistence like sunlight on skin that had lived too long in shade. Brotherhood sharpened me into resilience, and sometimes the blade nicked the parts of me I was learning to protect. There were seasons when their lessons clashed. Sisters urged me to soften. Brothers warned me to harden. The tug-of-war was real. Together, they gave me balance.

Long before the badge, there was another kind of brother, an older one from the detention center days, no badge then, just a presence that quieted a room. New York in his voice, the way he closed the distance, looked down at you with a half-smile, and spoke in a slow, low tone that made you listen. I do not remember seeing him angry. He loved the night shift—coaching—and he never needed to say he believed in you. You felt it in the way he stood near when the air changed. When grief knocked the wind out of me years later, I could still hear him: "Head up, kid. You are built for more than one bad day." Not tender, exactly, but true.

I carry both lessons now. Some days I lean on the brotherhood, the reminders to square my shoulders, to keep pushing, to endure. Other days I lean on the sisterhood—the reminders to slow down, to breathe, to let myself be held. They are not opposites. They are anchors that hold in different storms.

I came home brittle after one of those storms, the kind of tiredness that makes light feel loud. Kenzie was at the table, cutting out a paper crown. "You want to try it on me?" she asked. My first instinct was to say I had nothing left. Instead, I sat. She placed it on my head, fingers warm against my hairline. "You can be queen of resting," she said. I laughed, then let the laughter fall into tears. She did not flinch. She leaned her shoulder into mine until the shaking stopped. "Better?" "Better," I said, and meant it.

At every turn, what held me was not perfection or performance, but those three quiet words: I got you. They sounded different depending on where they came from, a sister pulling me close in a crowded restaurant, a line sister showing up when I didn't ask, a brother steadying me in the field with nothing more than a nudge and his spine against mine. The language shifted, but the promise was the same.

For a girl who learned early to carry everything alone—those words became proof that I didn't have to. They were anchors in chaos—reminders that love can be both soft and strong, both whispered in a hug and spoken through presence on a dangerous street.

That is the gift of family, chosen and found. Not that they erase the weight—but that when the weight threatens to crush you, someone leans in and says, "I got you." And sometimes, that is enough to keep going. But even love can't carry what you refuse to name.

The sisterhood and brotherhood held me steady, but the silence still lived under my skin. When the laughter faded and the radio crackled back to life, I felt the ache of what connection couldn't cure. The weight wasn't only in the streets; it followed me home.

CHAPTER 8

The Cracks Beneath the Badge

*The fractures hidden beneath a
uniform meant to protect*

THE VEST DUG INTO MY SHOULDERS before the sun was even up. Sweat already prickled my neck, and the silence of the house was louder than any siren. They never tell you how heavy the shield becomes. How the vest presses into your chest until you forget what ease feels like. Long nights blur together. The faces stay with you long after the call is over—eyes you can't unsee, voices that echo in quiet rooms. And when I went home, the weight didn't come off. It just changed shape.

The badge was heavy enough at work—the weight of decisions, of split seconds, of lives held in my hands. At home it carried something else. It carried silence, the quick glances when I walked through the door in uniform, the conversations that died before they reached me. I was both proof that we could belong, and proof that we never really would. Some nights, I wondered if the weight I carried was really protection at all, or just another kind of armor I couldn't take off.

The snap of my duty belt became the soundtrack of my mornings. Shirt. Vest. Belt. Click, snap, adjust. Each layer heavier than the one before. At the table, my daughter swung her legs, spoon tapping the rim of her cereal bowl. She watched me transform—Rashida fading, Officer Saunders emerging. Sometimes, so softly I almost missed it, she whispered, "Be safe, Mommy." I bent to kiss the crown of her head and said, "Always." It wasn't a guarantee.

Because the badge doesn't just rest on your chest, it seeps into you. It presses past fabric and skin until it feels like part of your bones. It rewrites the way your body carries fear, teaching muscles to brace before your mind has time to name the threat. My shoulders ached in ways even sleep couldn't repair, as if the job had rearranged my bones. Even laughter felt shallow—my lungs never filling all the way.

The vest carried a smell I could never wash out—the permanent musk of summers baked in sweat, winters carved by cold, Kevlar that never forgot its purpose. It was as if the fibers themselves had absorbed every cry, every scream—every danger I tried to leave behind. Even off duty, my body remembered. My posture leaned forward, always bracing. My eyes searched for exits without permission. Vigilance became a second skin I could never peel away.

Once, Kenzie drew me as a stick figure with a wide smile and a square badge scribbled across my chest. "That's you, Mommy. You're strong." I thanked her and tucked it into my bag, pretending the lump in my throat was just pride. She said it so easily, like strength was something simple, something worn instead of carried. To her, that badge meant courage, goodness, safety—the kind of safety I spent my days chasing for other people but could never seem to hold for myself.

I watched her beam, crayons scattered around her, and wondered what image she was really drawing—the mother she saw, or the one I was trying so hard to become. I smiled back, but inside I felt the quiet ache of someone who knew that strength often came with a cost no child should ever have to imagine. That night I stared at the paper badge and wondered if she'd still draw a smile if she knew what it cost—the sleepless nights, the hollow stares, the way my body flinched at sudden sounds, even when she was the one laughing. She saw strength where I felt only survival, and in her eyes, the uniform still meant safety, not the weight I carried inside it. Another time, she asked if my vest was like a superhero costume. I didn't have the heart to tell her it was closer to a shield I couldn't set down.

But it wasn't only Kenzie who reminded me why I carried the badge. Sometimes it was strangers. A random card slipped into the precinct mailbox, written in a child's uneven handwriting: *Thank you for keeping us safe.* Sometimes it was an older Black woman who stopped me outside a store, her face lit with a smile that carried more than words. "Baby, I'm glad to see you out here," she said, gripping my hand like she was blessing me. And sometimes it was the smallest things, little kids tugging at my vest to ask for stickers, or holding up their phones shyly to take a picture with me like I was somebody worth remembering. Those moments never lasted long, but they cut through the weight. They reminded me that the badge could mean presence, not just pressure.

Strangers called me brave. Family called me strong. Both sounded like praise, but both felt like pressure. Strong meant silent; brave meant unbreakable. Neither left room to be human. I performed composure until it fit tighter than my own skin. A calm voice over adrenaline. Steady hands over a tremor. A detached gaze over a breaking heart. Professionalism became a mask I wore so long I forgot where it ended and I began.

The weight never clocks out. You can hang the uniform in the closet, but it doesn't stay there. It follows you into the kitchen—settling heavy between dinner plates and half-finished conversations. It hums beneath the quiet, a low reminder that peace is something you have to relearn every night. The sound of silverware against porcelain can pull you back to sirens, to echoes you thought you'd buried. The body keeps score, even when the world says your shift is over.

It sinks into the couch on movie night, pressing against your side even as your child curls into you for comfort. It lingers at the edge of the bed, patient and unrelenting, watching as you lean over the soft rise and fall of your child's sleep. In those moments, the ache softens, but it never disappears. You learn to live beside it—to breathe through it—reminding yourself that even in gentleness, you are still learning how to be free from the grip of what you once carried home.

At restaurants, I never sat with my back to the door. In grocery stores, I scanned every aisle before reaching for the shelves. At the park, while Kenzie pumped her legs on the swing and called, "Higher, Mommy!" my eyes stayed on the parking lot. She laughed with abandon. I braced for a threat that never came. One afternoon, she paused mid-coloring, studied my face, and asked, "Why do you always look so serious?" I told her I was just thinking—but the truth was, *I was always scanning.* The job didn't just change my habits. It changed how I carried fear.

Some nights, grief came only when no one was watching. Parked in the dark, still sealed inside my uniform, I gripped the steering wheel until my knuckles burned. The tears came slow, stubborn, as if even they needed permission. The badge had taken more than it ever gave back.

In those moments, I could feel every weight I had carried—the voices, the violence, the faces that never left. I sat there until the silence grew heavy enough to break me open, and only then did I finally breathe.

I have walked into homes where children were bruised by the people meant to protect them. I have stood over bodies cooling too fast, the smell of blood and loss lingering long after the sirens faded. I have listened to mothers scream until their voices shredded, grief so heavy it choked the air and bent the room around it. I learned to stand still through it all, to quiet the tremor in my hands, to hold my breath until the chaos settled. That was the job. That was survival. And through it all, I was steady. That is what people saw.

What they did not see was how the weight came back later. At first it was quiet, then it became relentless. It hardened into a silence no one questioned. It spilled out sideways in sharp words that were not fair. That is what people saw. It lingered in the sleepless hours, my eyes locked on ceilings that never answered back, the quiet pressing heavy as the memories I refused to name.

The night began with a domestic violence call. The kind of quiet that only follows something terrible. A woman stood in the living room with her children pressed behind her like shadows. His arrest was routine; the paperwork was standard. As we led him out, one of the children whispered, "Don't let him come back." The smallness of his voice caught in my chest like barbed wire. I swallowed hard. *Don't cry here. Don't break here.* Not in uniform.

A few hours later came the welfare check, the kind that always made my stomach tighten. A young mother opened the door, eyes rimmed red. Her toddler had wandered outside while she was in the bathroom. It was not neglect; it was exhaustion. "I'm just so tired," she whispered—shame folding her frame in half. "You're doing your best," I told her, voice even. Inside, something caved. I was so tired too, and no one knew it. Her little boy peeked from behind her leg, and for a breath I saw Kenzie's face. My hand went to the wall to steady what my training told me to ignore.

The overdose call came just before dawn. A man slumped on linoleum, a needle near his hand. His teenage daughter knelt beside him, shaking his shoulders and whispering, "Daddy, wake up. Please, wake up." My partner started clearing the scene. I couldn't move—yet. The sound of her voice rooted me. In her pleading I heard an echo, the girl I used to be, writing letters to a father who never came. That "please" followed me for weeks: in the shower, at red lights, brushing Kenzie's hair. But the badge gave me a new way to hide—a polished armor that looked like purpose but felt like isolation. I wore it with pride, convincing myself it made me whole, when in truth it was hollowing me out from the inside. Every salute, every steady nod, every call I answered—another layer between who I was and who I pretended to be. The badge didn't just protect me; it disguised my breaking.

Still, the job was not only about the calls. It was about the climate the badge existed in. Headlines. Footage on loop. Protests. Sideways glances that asked me to defend the uniform I wore and the Black skin beneath it. Some days it felt like carrying two wars: one against the weight of the work, and one against the assumptions of the world. One shift, I was thanked as an officer; that night, I was cursed as a traitor. To some, my badge erased my Blackness. To others, my Blackness erased the badge. Either way, I was left carrying the weight of both.

At home, the waiting worked quietly. I sat at dinner while conversation moved around me, nodding at Kenzie's stories as my mind replayed someone else's tragedy. The laughter at the table felt distant, like it belonged to another life. I tried to anchor myself in her voice, in the warmth of her small hands waving through another story, but the noise of the day still hummed beneath my skin. Later, she would tug my sleeve—"Mommy, you're not listening." She was right. My body was home. My mind was still out there, somewhere between the sirens and the silence that followed.

One night I dropped my duty belt on the table and the thud traveled through the house like a warning. Kenzie reached for the metal she had seen on my hips a thousand times. "Can I hold it, Mommy?" she asked. My chest tightened. "Not this, baby," I said—pulling it back. She frowned, confused. "But it's yours." And that is when I understood. The badge was not only mine. Its weight was already reaching for her. Some nights the silence felt like a hand-me-down, another version of my mother's survival: chin high, feelings swallowed. But the badge gave me a new way to hide—a polished armor that looked like purpose but felt like isolation. I wore it with pride, convincing myself it made me whole, when in truth it was hollowing me out from the inside. Every salute, every steady nod, every call I answered became another layer between who I was and who I pretended to be. The badge didn't just protect me; it disguised my breaking.

Therapy was the first place I began to pry it loose. I sat stiff, arms crossed, the old silence hardened in place. "When's the last time you cried?" my therapist asked. "I don't remember," I lied. My body remembered—the ache in my chest, the tightness in my throat. Weeks later, the truth slipped out—barely audible: "This job is breaking me." Shame rose and then relief. If it was real, maybe it could be healed.

More than once I sat in my car after a shift, fingers hovering over the ignition, imagining what it would feel like if I just did not go back. Not tonight. Not ever. But each time I started the engine anyway, breaking a little more in the process. Slowly, I began to mourn the parts of me that had gone quiet, almost without my noticing. The girl who once cried at movies—without shame. The woman who laughed too loud, head thrown back, unafraid of being heard. The mother who dreamed her daughter would inherit joy instead of vigilance—softness instead of armor.

Piece by piece, I realized how much of myself I had buried just to keep functioning. In that room I finally said the words I could not say anywhere else: "I don't know who I am without it." The confession fell into the air like glass breaking. The silence that followed terrified me more than any call I had ever been on, because calls end but silence lingers, and I feared it meant there was nothing left beneath the badge. Then another truth surfaced, small, steady, almost ordinary, but strong enough to hold onto. Real strength is not measured by how much weight you can carry. Real strength is knowing when something is crushing you and daring to set it down.

The world will never see the cost written in the margins of our reports, but I feel it every day in my bones, in the startle that will not leave, in the fragments I buried just to keep moving. The badge gave me authority. It also deepened my silence. It gave me a role. It asked for pieces in return. And the question grew louder: If I am not the badge, who am I? Louder still: *What will my daughter inherit if I don't find the answer?*

The danger is not always out there. Sometimes it's the silence you carry inside—the grief you fold into corners, the wounds you tend alone.

It teaches you to smile through ache, to mistake composure for peace. But even the strongest armor begins to crack when the heart has nowhere left to rest.

The badge taught me how to survive, how to endure, how to keep moving when everything in me wanted to stop. But survival was never the finish line. My daughter is the reason I remembered I was meant for more than endurance. She is the reason I remembered I was meant to live, fully and openly, with laughter that does not shrink and love that doesn't hide.

It followed me through the front door, settling into every corner of my house—a quiet shadow that refused to stay behind. I carried it to the dinner table, where conversation faltered under its heaviness, into bedtime routines, where my smile strained to hide the day, even into my daughter's laughter, where joy met a kind of exhaustion I couldn't yet name. No matter how hard I tried to leave it in the locker, the truth was this: I was carrying it all home.

CHAPTER 9

Armor That Followed Me Home

The defenses I carried long
after the work was done

THE BADGE CAME HOME WITH me, but so did my daughter's laughter. And even when my body braced for war in the silence of night, her joy reminded me there was more to live for than survival. The world thought my shift ended when the uniform was hung in my locker. But the truth was, I never clocked out. The armor followed me, into my daughter's laughter, into my partner's bed, into phone calls with my family I didn't have the patience to answer. Even without the badge on my chest, my body still braced for impact.

One night it proved clearer than any other. Crack. The sound tore through the quiet. Fireworks, maybe. Fun fire, people called it. But to me, it was a gunshot. My body didn't wait for permission. Before thought could catch up, I was already on the floor, crawling toward Kenzie's room like my life depended on it. Knees slammed hard. Breath jagged in my throat, lungs refusing to fill.

Behind me, the sheets rustled. "What the— Rashida, are you okay?" His voice was groggy, tangled with concern, but it barely reached me. My chest heaved, my heart pounding so loud it drowned out everything else. The floor was cold beneath my cheek, grounding me just enough to know I wasn't back there—but my body didn't believe it. My breath came in sharp bursts, my mind looping through the flash of light, the sound, the silence that followed. I wanted to answer, to say I was fine, but the truth was I was somewhere else entirely.

Back at that traffic stop. Muzzle flash. My partner shouting commands I couldn't hear. My own pulse roaring like thunder. My body didn't care that this was a bedroom. It only knew survival.

When I finally turned my head, he was watching me—confusion, worry, helplessness etched across his face. Panic gave way to something even worse: shame. He had seen me break. Seen how the armor lived in me even here, in the one place it should have fallen away. "I'm fine," I whispered, the lie bitter on my tongue. Because the truth was unbearable: even in the safety of his arms, my instinct was to leave him behind and crawl toward danger. Toward whatever needed saving. And that gutted me most.

The morning after, we didn't talk about it. He asked again, softer this time, if I was alright. I nodded, poured my coffee, and pretended to be distracted by the news on TV. He watched me for a long time across the kitchen table, like he wanted to press but didn't know how. I felt his gaze on me, heavy as the vest I thought I'd left behind. I stared into my mug, ashamed of how badly I wanted him to stop asking. Silence felt safer than being known. But silence didn't erase what he saw. It only made the distance thicker.

If my partner saw the cracks, Kenzie lived inside them. Children don't need words to know when the armor is there. They just feel it. They translate it. They bend themselves around it. At the park, while she begged me to push her higher, my eyes scanned the parking lot. The screech of tires tightened my chest. A man lingering near the swings locked my stare, suspicion rising before reason could catch up. "Higher, Mommy! Higher!" she laughed, legs kicking wide. But

I couldn't give her higher when my body was already rehearsing how I'd shield her if it came to that.

At the grocery store, she skipped down the aisle, her laughter bouncing off shelves lined with cereal boxes and canned soup. I kept one hand on the cart, the other tightening unconsciously around the handle as my eyes darted from face to face. A man's jacket bulged near his hip, and my body stilled before my mind could reason. My breath caught, waiting—was it a weapon, or just a phone? Around me, life moved on as if nothing had changed, but inside me, the sirens were already blaring. She tugged a box of cereal off the shelf, smiling wide, her small joy cutting through the hum of the store. "Put that back," I snapped before I even realized my voice had risen. Her smile crumpled, confusion clouding the light in her eyes. I wanted to take the words back, to soften them somehow, but my body was still in defense mode, my gaze locked on the stranger's pocket. I was present and gone all at once—a mother in a grocery aisle, a cop still waiting for danger to reveal itself.

At home, it was the same. On movie nights she tugged at my sleeve when she caught me staring past the screen, eyes fixed on the door like it might explode open at any second. "Watch, Mommy," she whispered, trying to pull me back. And one afternoon, while coloring, she looked up and asked, "Why do you always look mad, Mommy?" Her question split me wide open. I wasn't mad. I was scared. Exhausted. *Elsewhere.* But how do you explain hypervigilance to a child? How do you tell her that your face, your silence, your stillness are not anger at her but fear of everything else?

She leaned against me then, her small hand resting on my arm. For a moment my body stilled, not in fear but in something closer to peace. Her warmth reminded me that I was still here, still hers, even if my mind was elsewhere. Later that night she made me laugh, really laugh, by twirling around the living room until she tumbled onto the couch in a heap. For a split second the armor loosened. It was proof that joy could still find its way through the cracks.

Most nights, I couldn't let go. I would park in the driveway and sit there in silence, gripping the steering wheel until my fingers hurt. Some nights tears came fast and hot, spilling before I could wipe them away. I sat there until my face cooled, afraid to let Kenzie see the weight I carried inside. By the time I opened the front door, the mask was back in place. She deserved better, but too often I gave her only distance wrapped in routine.

Children don't just notice. They adapt. Kenzie learned when to be quiet, when to pull me back, when to try harder to make me laugh. She learned to tiptoe around my tension like it was furniture in the room. And I hated it. Because I knew exactly what she was doing. I had done the same for my own mother.

Sometimes she even tried to protect me. She would double-check the locks on the doors, peek through the blinds like she had seen me do, or shush her cousins when she thought the noise might make me snap. Once she even asked if she should "watch the windows" so I could finish dinner in peace. She was a child, yet already learning to play sentry, rehearsing safety instead of innocence. That realization crushed me.

The armor showed up in smaller ways too. At restaurants I insisted on facing the door, never letting my back be exposed. In movie theaters I chose the aisle seat, eyes flicking from screen to exits every few minutes. Even at home, I found myself rehearsing escape routes, mentally charting where we'd run if the unthinkable happened. These were not choices; they were instincts. But to Kenzie, they looked like distance. To her, it must have felt like I was always one step away, never fully there. It wasn't just Kenzie who felt the weight. My family carried it too.

After long shifts, my body was wrecked. Feet swollen and throbbing. Shoulders locked. Ears still carrying the squawk of radios. I'd stand in the doorway, peeling off the vest, unbuckling the duty belt, each piece clattering to the floor like I was shedding skin. The armor beneath stayed: posture, suspicion, silence. By the time the phone rang, I was emptied out. "Rashida, you listening?" my sister asked once, frustration cutting through her tone. "Yeah, I'm here," I muttered. "No, you're not," she shot back, and she was right.

I remember one call in particular. She was telling me about her day, an event she attended, about something that had made her laugh. I tried to keep up, but my mind was replaying a call from earlier, the sound of a mother's scream after losing her son. My sister's laughter felt like it was coming from another planet. When she asked if I was okay, I snapped: "I'm just tired, alright?" The silence on the line was thick, her hurt loud even without words.

If my sister noticed the silence, my mother knew it by heart. Her calls weren't much different. She told me about bills, about work, about the news. To her, it was connection. To me, it was static against steel. I cut her short, muttered responses, waited for the call to end. And then came the guilt. Always the guilt.

I hated myself for it, for being sharp, for giving my patience to strangers and my sharpest edges to the people who loved me most. They deserved the daughter, the sister, the soft version of me I could no longer reach. I wanted to give it to them, but I didn't know how. The badge had trained me to hold it all, never to be held. So when they pressed too close, I pulled the armor tighter, terrified they'd see how close I was to unraveling.

The truth is, the weight I carried wasn't just professional. It was cultural. Black women are taught early that softness is dangerous, that tears are weakness, that the world already has its foot on our necks and no one is coming to rescue us. We swallow it, we harden, we armor up before anyone hands us a badge. By the time I put on the uniform, I was already fluent in silence. Law enforcement just gave it another name. I had seen the women around me, aunties and neighbors, carry it too. Their voices sharp when the bills piled up. Their shoulders squared as if rest was a luxury they couldn't afford. In church, we dressed in our Sunday best and called it joy, even when our hearts were breaking. We performed strength because we didn't believe softness could keep us alive.

And if silence marked my calls with them, it became a chasm with my brother. His first incarceration hurt but didn't surprise me. Where I grew up, it was almost expected. I wrote letters anyway, careful with every word, stuffing hope into envelopes I barely believed in. I'm proud of you. Hold on. Lies, maybe, but it was all I had to give. The second time broke me. His sentence was longer. The loss sharper. I still remember my mom's voice on the phone, flat, tired, like air leaking from a balloon. "They gave him more this time," she said. Her sigh collapsed against the receiver. Her silence after carried more weight than her words. *His absence reshaped every one of us.*

I told myself anger was easier. Easier to be mad than to admit how much I missed him. Easier to say I didn't care than to risk losing him again. One night, I sat at the kitchen table with a pen hovering over paper. The letter started: I miss you. I'm scared for you. I don't know how to hold this without you here. My hand shook. I shoved it into a drawer, unfinished, unsent. That drawer became a coffin. Every letter left inside was another shovelful of dirt over a relationship I swore I didn't need. But I did. God, I did. And I hated myself for needing someone the world had already written off.

Sometimes I'd pull the drawer open just to look at the paper, the half-formed words staring back at me like ghosts. I couldn't bring myself to finish them. Couldn't bring myself to send them. I left them there, buried. And with every unsent letter, the distance grew wider, the silence heavier, until it felt easier to pretend he was gone than admit how much I wanted him back. I wondered then if Kenzie would one day open a drawer of her own, filled with words she never said to me. What silence was I passing down to her?

Years later, I finally sent him one. It wasn't long, just a few sentences scratched out after midnight. I don't know how to do this right, but I want to try again. I love you. I miss you. I thought my hand might break writing the words, but once I mailed it, I felt something shift. Small, but real. Forgiveness didn't erase the hurt, but it split the shield just enough to see him as more than his worst mistakes.

Even now, letting him back in feels dangerous. Not because I don't love him, but because love asks me to lay down the armor I've worn for so long. And laying it down means risk. It means trusting that the hands reaching for me won't turn cold. In that quiet realization, I saw the truth more clearly than before. This was never just my story. Silence had been our inheritance, passed from one heart to the next, teaching us how to survive but not how to stay open.

I thought about my mother. The way she smoked cigarettes in silence, exhaling fury she never spoke. The way her voice turned sharp when the weight got too heavy. The way her shoulders squared against the world like softness was a luxury she couldn't afford. I thought about my grandmother before her, slamming doors, holding secrets, chin high like the world owed her nothing. The inheritance wasn't money or land. It was armor. We passed it down like family heirlooms, jaw clenched, eyes hard, hearts guarded. And now here I was, watching my daughter bend around my silence, already preparing to carry the same weight.

And that was the part that haunted me more than bullets ever did. I could survive the job. I could survive the silence. But if I passed it on to her, if my daughter grew up believing distance was love and vigilance was safety, then all of it would have been for nothing. If I didn't face that question, the armor would live in me forever. And worse, it would live in her.

One night I sat on the edge of the bed. I realized then that silence wasn't protecting me. It was swallowing me, piece by piece, until I could barely recognize my own voice. The badge was heavy, but it wasn't the only weight I carried. The harder part was learning how to set it down, to stop measuring my worth by how much I could hold. I couldn't let that be her inheritance. I wanted my daughter to know a love that didn't come wrapped in armor. The badge didn't create the armor; it simply gave it a name, a purpose, a reason to keep hiding behind strength. And when the noise finally quieted, when there was no one left to save but myself, I was left with the question I had spent years avoiding. Who am I without it—without the armor, without the noise?

CHAPTER 10

Who Was I Without the Badge?

The role I wore and the self I almost lost

THE BADGE DIDN'T CREATE THE ARMOR, it simply gave it a name. I let it define me, holding it like proof that I mattered, like the only thing standing between who I was and who I feared becoming again. I used to run my fingers over the grooves before every shift, reminding myself of what it meant to serve, to show up, to stand in the gap. It became second skin. Until one day, I took it off and felt something stranger than loss—I felt exposed. Who was I without it—without the shine, the authority stitched to my chest, the quick respect it demanded before I even spoke? Who was I when the vest came off, when the badge lay silent on the dresser, when there was no uniform left to hide behind?

There's one night I'll never forget. It made the headlines—but the story they told wasn't the one that stayed with me. What the public saw was an officer doing her job. What I remember is how that night tore something open inside me. It didn't end in tragedy, but it changed me in a way I never came back from. That night marked the beginning of a question I would spend years trying to answer. It was early in my career, when adrenaline still felt like courage. My partner and I responded to a domestic violence call, one of thousands I would go on to handle. The caller's voice trembled through the radio. Her partner was drunk, possibly suicidal, reportedly armed with a rifle. No detailed call history. No time to prepare. Just lights, sirens, and instinct pushing us forward.

When we pulled up, the silence was eerie. Too quiet. Too still. The kind of silence that makes your stomach knot before your mind catches up. The front door was wide open, porch light spilling long shadows across the lawn. A television flickered blue through the blinds, but no voices, no movement. We moved with caution, split the approach, scanned windows, radios crackling at a whisper. My vest pressed heavy against my chest, sweat already pooling beneath the straps though the night was cool. Every sound sharpened, the crunch of gravel under my boots, the buzz of a streetlamp overhead, the pounding of blood in my ears. It was routine until it wasn't. Pop. Pop-pop—gunfire.

The sound tore through the quiet. For a split second, I didn't process it. Was it warning? Was it aimed? My body didn't wait for answers. I dropped behind a car, my palms raw against the asphalt, adrenaline roaring like fire through my chest. My hand gripped my weapon so hard my knuckles ached. For a moment, there was nothing but my heartbeat. The world shrank to a single thought: *You could die right here.*

I've never served in the military, but that night I understood war. A war zone in the middle of a quiet cul-de-sac. Porch lights glowing, wind chimes swaying, and in the middle of it all, chaos. Fear so thick it sat in my throat like smoke. I remember the smallest details, the peeling paint on the front door, the smell of wet grass, my partner's sharp breath over the radio. Trauma records everything. Seconds dragged like hours. Then headlights, voices, boots pounding pavement. Backup arrived. Orders were shouted, negotiations began. No one was killed. The man was arrested. And like always, we cleared the scene, completed the paperwork, and moved on.

But I didn't move on. That night followed me home. The echoes of gunfire lived in my chest, rattling against my ribs long after the scene was cleared. In the shower, steam filled the room while phantom shots cracked through memory, the sound bouncing off tile and bone. I tried to wash the night away, but it clung to me, invisible and heavy. Sleep became shallow, a negotiation I rarely won. I jolted awake at every creak of the house, heart pounding before I even opened my eyes. Even the sound of my daughter dropping a toy sent a tremor through me, my body reacting before my mind could remember we were safe.

I told myself it was nothing, just a bad night. But the truth was quieter and harder to face. Part of me had stayed out there, somewhere between the flashing lights and the fear I never learned how to put down. The call ended on paper—but in my body, it never did. That's the part no one tells you. The badge comes off, but the hypervigilance doesn't. The fear, the survival scenarios looping in your head, they follow you everywhere. I carried it quietly, told myself I was fine. But "fine" is the lie officers tell until the cracks show. My body told the truth instead—clenched jaw, shallow sleep, shoulders that never learned to drop.

Therapy was the first place I admitted it—to myself and anyone else. I didn't go easily. Where I come from, and in the job I held, therapy wasn't where you went. You prayed. You poured a drink. You stuffed it down and kept moving. Sitting across from a stranger and talking about fear felt like weakness. It felt like betrayal of the armor I had been taught to wear. I almost turned around in the parking lot. My pride told me I didn't need it. But something heavier than pride pulled me inside. Walking into therapy felt harder than crouching behind that patrol car. At least out there, I knew the rules of survival. In that room, I had to invent new ones.

My therapist asked me to close my eyes and just breathe. I tried. My jaw locked. My shoulders stayed high. Breathing itself felt like danger. My body screamed: If you relax, you won't be ready. If you're not ready, you won't survive. But slowly, something shifted. My fists softened; my breath dropped lower into my belly. The air finally reached a part of me it hadn't touched in years. My body remembered, just for a moment, what it felt like to not be braced.

That moment taught me something important: healing doesn't always begin with words. Sometimes it begins by remembering how to exhale. Weeks later, I finally said the word "fear" out loud, my voice cracking like the first shot of gunfire. My therapist nodded, no judgment, no rush. For the first time, I wasn't crushed under the silence of it.

The badge gives you access, authority, identity. It tells the world who you are, but it can also make you forget. I didn't realize how much of myself I had folded into the job, how much of my worth I had tied to being the strong one. Every call, every report, every uniform inspection became proof that I was in control, that I was needed, that I mattered. Somewhere along the way, I started believing the badge and I were the same. The badge became my armor, the thing I hid behind when I didn't know how to be vulnerable. It protected me from what I didn't have the words to name, but it also kept me at a distance from everything that made me human. Over time, it became a mask. It was easier to be the officer than the woman underneath. Easier to show up for everyone else than to admit I was running on empty.

It's hard to explain what "to protect and serve" means when you're a Black officer. It isn't just a motto; it's a tightrope. Every day you're balancing the duty to protect a community that mirrors your own reflection while wearing a system that hasn't always protected people who look like you. You carry the weight of the uniform and the burden of representation at the same time. At the academy, they trained us on tactics, law, and procedure. They taught us how to clear a room, read danger, stay alive. But they never said what it would cost to live in two worlds at once. No one mentioned the weight of softening your tone so you wouldn't be seen as a threat, or straightening your posture to earn respect that should've already been given. They never warned us how exhausting it would be to adjust your smile, your language, your entire presence just to survive both sides. After a while, you start to forget which version of yourself came first—the one behind the badge, or the one who put it on.

They never trained us for that. They never trained us for the suspicion in the eyes of a child who looked like my own family. They never trained us for the silence in briefing rooms when I raised a concern, or for the stares that said I didn't quite belong in the blue or the Black. I'll never forget one night after a long shift. A man in the neighborhood I grew up in looked at me and shook his head. "You forgot where you came from," he muttered. Hours later at work, a colleague joked that I must have gotten the job because of "diversity numbers." Too blue for some—too Black for others. I laughed it off in the moment, but when I got home, the words stung like shrapnel. They carried more than insult. They carried the loneliness of never being enough for either side.

For me, protecting and serving was never just about protocol. It was about compassion. About looking a young Black boy in the eye and silently saying: You matter, even if the system doesn't reflect it. But compassion doesn't erase the tension. And the line between who I was and what the job demanded blurred so often I couldn't always tell where the badge ended and I began.

I remember a day off after a stretch of heavy shifts. No radio, no calls, no briefing. Just quiet. I should have rested, but instead I paced the house, folding laundry that didn't need folding, checking my phone for messages that weren't coming. The walls felt too close, the silence too sharp. My body didn't know how to be still. It was trained to respond, to move, to fix. I stood by the window watching the street, waiting for something—anything—to pull me back into purpose. But nothing came. Only the sound of my own breathing and the hum of a life that had learned to run on alert. The restlessness settled deep in my chest, pressing against the question I could no longer ignore. Who am I when no one needs saving—when no one calls my name?

Saving people had become part of my worth. The calls, the interventions, the arrests, they all whispered that I mattered because someone needed me. Without that need, who was I? That question haunted me in small ways too. I'll never forget leaving a community event in plain clothes. A man I'd worked with for years walked right past me without recognition. No nod. No hello. Just nothing. And it hit me: *Am I only visible when I'm wearing the badge?*

That thought followed me home. I carried it like another kind of weight. That night, I sat on the couch replaying the moment, invisibility pressing heavy on my chest. My daughter climbed into my lap, tugging at my sweatshirt. "Why are you sad, Mommy?" she asked, her eyes wide, unfiltered. She didn't care that I wasn't in uniform. She didn't need the badge to see me. To her, I was already enough. She saw her mother first. Rashida first. And in that moment I realized: the people who matter most don't need proof stitched to your chest. They just need you—whole, human, present.

I thought of all the mornings I kissed her forehead before leaving for work. Her hair still warm from sleep, her breath soft against my cheek. Sometimes she whispered, "Be safe, Mommy." Those three words carried both faith and fear. She was too young to name it, but she knew the uniform meant danger. Still, it never changed how she saw me. She didn't see the badge or the headlines or the exhaustion I tried to hide. She saw the person beneath it all. To her, I was still just Mommy—the safe place, the steady heartbeat, the one who always came home. That kind of love is its own truth. A mirror I didn't know I needed. In her eyes, I saw the woman I'd started to lose under the weight of the job. For a moment, I remembered who I was before the armor, before the silence, before the badge became the story.

But when the noise faded and the world got quiet again, I realized how much of myself I had given away to being needed. And yet, isolation became my teacher. In the stillness, I could no longer hide behind the noise or the badge. Without the constant pull of being needed, I was forced to face the parts of me I had neglected—the woman beneath the uniform, the heart beneath the armor. It was uncomfortable, almost unbearable at first. The silence pressed against everything I'd used to define myself. It forced me to ask whether belonging really meant squeezing myself into spaces where I'd never fit, or silencing truths that made others comfortable. For so long, I had mistaken being needed for being known. I called it purpose, but sometimes it was survival, a way to avoid my own emptiness. Slowly, I began to understand—real belonging wasn't about being useful, being chosen, or being strong enough to hold everyone else together. It was about creating spaces where I didn't have to shrink. It was learning that I was still whole—even when no one called my name.

One afternoon, I walked into a community event in plain clothes. No radio, no vest, no badge. Just me. The air smelled like hot cocoa and cardboard boxes. Children's laughter bounced off the walls, parents held bags of groceries, volunteers moved with steady rhythm. I stood on the edge, nervous. Without my uniform, did I still belong?

Then a woman I had helped years ago spotted me. Her face lit up, and she crossed the room. She hugged me tight and said, "You're the one who showed up for us." Not the officer. Not the badge. *Me.* Her words settled into me like truth I had been waiting to believe. Identity isn't erased when the uniform comes off. It expands. The badge may always be part of my story—but it isn't the whole of me.

These days, I don't run my fingers over the grooves of the badge to remember who I am. I press my hand to my chest, feel my own heartbeat, and know: I was whole all along. When my daughter whispers, "Be safe, Mommy," I know safety isn't just about surviving the street. It's about being present enough to come home as myself. When I walk into a community room in plain clothes, I remind myself: *showing up as Rashida is enough.*

I may never fully silence the echoes of gunfire or erase the weight of the armor. But I have learned to live with them without letting them define me. The badge may be part of my story, but my heartbeat is my proof. And for Kenzie, that heartbeat has always been enough. She never needed the badge or the weight it carried, only the sound of me coming home. In her eyes, I wasn't a protector or a symbol. I was simply her mother, the one who showed up, who loved her back to safety with steady hands and a soft voice.

That's the uniform I'll never take off. The one stitched from love, from presence, from everything that outlasts duty. She became my reminder that I was more than what I did, that love is its own kind of service—and sometimes the hardest kind to stay faithful to. Love has a way of revealing what protection hides—what armor conceals. It asks for softness where armor once lived, and courage where silence once stood. It opens the door to everything I had kept waiting—the ache, the joy, and the longing in between.

PART III

Love, Loss, and the Longing Between

*The embers of joy, the shadows of grief,
the ache of in-between*

Love promised safety and sometimes delivered
pain. Grief came without warning and stayed
without permission.

Between them stretched a longing I did not
know how to name, a hunger for tenderness that
could outlast the silence.

CHAPTER 11

What Motherhood Revealed

*The tenderness uncovered by tiny hands
and unguarded trust*

MOTHERHOOD DIDN'T ARRIVE IN A NEAT PACKAGE, tied with certainty or stability. It came through a complicated love. Kenzie's father and I were never simple. We loved each other, but love wasn't enough to keep us steady. Still, his presence shaped the beginning of motherhood for me—he gave me a daughter who would change everything, though we could not last.

Kenzie was only three when she first showed me myself. I sank onto the edge of the bed, the weight of the day pressing heavy across my shoulders, my body tired from the wear and tear of the shift. Our home was dim, the air thick with the kind of silence that usually felt like relief after long hours on patrol. But that night, it pressed against me like a truth I wasn't ready to face. I leaned forward, elbows on my knees, staring at the floor, trying to steady my breath. The tears burned behind my eyes. I thought I was hidden enough, quiet enough, armored enough. But grief has a way of slipping through even the strongest steel.

Then I heard it. The slap of tiny feet against the floor. Her huge afro was pulled back into a loose ponytail, her blanket dragging behind her, still heavy with sleep. Without hesitation, she climbed into my lap, small body warm against mine. She reached up, pressed her palm to my cheek, and whispered, "Don't cry, Mommy."

Her voice was soft, but it carried a steadiness that stunned me. Almost as if she were giving me permission I had never given myself—to fall apart. My instinct was to pull away, to swallow the tears, to replace them with the practiced smile that said I'm fine. But her hand stayed there, soft and insistent, holding me in a way that made hiding impossible. In her wide, unflinching eyes, I wasn't a badge or a burden or someone who had to hold it all together. I was just her mother. And for once, someone reached for me not in admiration of my strength, but in recognition of my breaking.

That night I learned a truth I hadn't been ready for: *motherhood reveals what silence hides*. I hadn't realized how much of myself I had buried until Kenzie reflected it back to me. She didn't see someone who had to be perfect. She saw someone worth loving, even in pieces. And in her reflection, I saw the ache of my own childhood, the parts of me that had wanted to be noticed, to be held, to be met without having to earn it.

That realization pulled me backward, toward my own mother. I remembered flashes of her love: the rare nights when she tickled us until we couldn't breathe, her laughter spilling out like something she rarely let the world hear. For those moments, joy filled the house, wild and uncontained. My sides would ache, my cheeks wet with tears from laughing too hard, and for a few minutes it felt like love had cracked the silence wide open.

It never lasted. The laughter always dissolved into quiet, as if joy had overstayed its welcome. I remember lying in bed afterward, chest still heaving from giggles, holding my breath as the house slipped back into stillness. That's how I learned to ration joy the way we rationed food or electricity. Love came in pieces, fleeting and fragile, never promised to stay.

Where my mother rationed joy, Kenzie demanded it. She hadn't yet learned that tenderness could be withheld. When she laughed, she expected me to laugh with her. When she cried, she expected to be held. She lived by a rhythm that startled me, open hands, open heart, unapologetic need. And every time she reached, she revealed how much I had been longing for the same.

Her presence interrupted me in ways I didn't expect. When she collapsed into a tantrum, my instinct was to silence her, to steer her toward composure the way I had once been steered. The urge rose up quickly: *stop crying, toughen up, be strong.* The very script I had memorized as a child. But something in me resisted.

I remembered what it felt like to swallow tears in the dark, to ache for someone to notice. So instead of snapping at her, I bent down and picked her up. I held her while she screamed, rubbed her back, whispered, "You're safe. I'm here." The words felt foreign at first, almost borrowed. But with each repetition, they became my own. That's the truth no one tells you about breaking cycles: it feels clumsy, awkward, like speaking a language with an accent that betrays you. But Kenzie didn't care if my words stumbled. She cared that I said them. That I stayed.

Her lessons grew louder as she grew older. She was about seven when she caught me in a lie I didn't even realize I was telling. I had just come home from another shift, shoulders sagging, the smell of the streets still clinging to me. She was at the kitchen table, crayons scattered everywhere, humming as she filled a page with color.

"Mommy, are you okay?" she asked, looking up.

"I'm fine," I answered quickly, sharp with muscle memory. The same mask I wore at work. The same mask I had learned in childhood. Fine. Always fine.

But she tilted her head, studying me with that fearless honesty only children possess. "You don't look fine," she said matter-of-factly. Her tone wasn't accusing. Just steady, like she was naming the color of the sky.

I froze, caught in the simple truth she had named. My instinct was to argue, to joke, to deflect. But her eyes stayed on me, waiting. And I realized she was giving me what my younger self had never been given: permission to be seen. I let the words slip out, halting and uneven. "Actually, baby… today was hard."

She nodded like it was the most ordinary thing in the world. Then, she pushed a crayon toward me. "You can color with me if you want." No lecture. No fix. Just presence. Even with my badge still heavy on my hip, she didn't need Officer Saunders. She wanted her mother. And that reminder something open in me again, not with tears, but with relief. She was teaching me that sometimes love didn't need answers. It only needed honesty and a place at the table.

One night, the mirror cut sharper. It had been a brutal shift. A domestic call where a child, no older than Kenzie, stood barefoot on the porch as we pulled up, her face streaked with tears, her little fists balled at her sides.

Kenzie was waiting. She was older now, maybe ten, perched on the couch with her homework spread across the cushions. She looked up when I walked in, studying my face the way she always did. I opened my mouth to greet her, but nothing came out. The words caught in my throat, the silence pressing heavier than the badge at my waist.

She tilted her head, her eyes narrowing with recognition. Then she did something that jolted me, she looked back down, mimicking the silence I was offering. In that moment, I saw it. The cycle replaying itself in real time. My silence teaching her silence, the same way my mother's had taught me. And for a split second, I almost let it happen.

But the fear of it, the terror of raising another child who learned to hold her tongue, to ration her tenderness, was stronger than the silence itself. I dropped onto the couch beside her, the metal of my duty belt digging into my side. My voice cracked when I finally forced it out. "Today was rough, baby."

She didn't say much, just leaned her head against my arm and kept her pencil moving across the page. The soft scratch of graphite filled the silence, steady and sure, grounding me in the simplest kind of peace. That small lean spoke more than words ever could. It was forgiveness without language, love without demand. In that moment, I felt the cycle crack. I had chosen presence over absence, softness over distance. The badge still clung to me, its weight not easily shed, but for the first time, I wasn't leading with it. I was leading with her. My words, when they finally came, were clumsy and unsure, but they didn't need to be perfect. She already understood. In that quiet, I realized that reaching didn't always mean speaking. Sometimes it simply meant staying—allowing love to fill the space that silence once guarded.

It was in those ordinary moments of tantrums, tears, and crayons on the table that extraordinary lessons took root. Little by little, she became my teacher. She showed me how to sit still when my instinct was to keep moving. She showed me that love wasn't only provision; it was presence. It was lying on the carpet beside her, stacking blocks and letting her knock them down just to hear her laugh. It was slowing down to read the same book five times in a row, her head pressed against my chest, her breath syncing with mine. It was letting her see me tired, messy, imperfect, and still letting her draw close.

Every time she reached for me, she chipped away at the armor I thought I couldn't take off. Her small hands didn't know the weight they were lifting—the years of silence, the layers of fear, the reflex to brace before being touched. With every hug, every burst of laughter that spilled between us, something in me softened. The badge had taught me how to protect, but she was teaching me how to be seen.

But here is what scared me most: I wasn't sure I could love her the way she deserved. I didn't have a blueprint for tenderness. No map for presence. Only scraps of inherited silence and a laugh that always ended too soon. What if I failed her the way silence had failed me? What if I taught her the very absence I was trying to escape? That was the weight I carried, heavier than the badge, more terrifying than any call I had answered. The fear that my silence could leak into hers. And yet even fear became a teacher.

Parenting revealed a truth I had overlooked: what I gave her would become what she carried. My silence would teach her silence. My softness would teach her softness. That is the thing about raising children, you are not just raising them, you are raising a mirror. And one day, they will hold it up to you. In raising her, I began re-raising myself. Each time I whispered you are safe, you are loved, I was speaking to the younger me who had ached for those words. Each hug loosened something that had been tight for decades. Each affirmation rewrote a silence I had carried since childhood.

Motherhood didn't erase my armor, but it cracked it wide enough for light to get in. Kenzie showed me that survival wasn't the only inheritance. That love could be louder than silence. That joy didn't have to dissolve back into stillness. That presence could be more powerful than protection. And that softness, the very thing I once feared would make me weak, was the only thing that could make me whole. Her reflection didn't just reshape how I mothered. It reshaped how I remembered being mothered.

I never wanted another mother. I only wanted mine. Thorns and tenderness, together. I love her sharp edges, her oversensitivity, her survival instincts. I know she wanted to keep me safe, to make sure I could stand when she no longer could. I did not always love that she gave me charley horses instead of hugs, but I understand now, that was her version of touch, the only way she knew how to reach. It wasn't the softness I craved, but it was still love, offered in the language she had.

Being a mother forced me to see my own mother differently, not as a failure, but as someone who gave all she could from what she had been given. Motherhood was the hardest thing I have ever done. Harder than carrying a badge. Harder than standing in chaos with a straight face. Policing demanded toughness. Parenting demanded transformation. It asked me not just to protect, but to soften, to risk closeness, to relearn what love could sound and feel like.

So I will say this as plainly as I can. Parents, don't give up on your children. And children, don't give up on your parents. There will be anger, disappointment, and silence that stretches too far. There will be moments when love feels one-sided, and forgiveness feels like surrender. But pause long enough to ask about the childhood that shaped them—the wounds they learned to hide, the lessons that taught them survival more than softness. You may not be able to excuse everything, and you shouldn't have to. But if you listen closely enough, you might begin to see the story beneath the behavior. You might find grief where you once saw indifference, fear where you assumed distance, love that never learned how to speak. And sometimes, that small shift in understanding becomes the first crack in the wall between you. Not absolution, but empathy. Not erasure, but a door toward healing.

Motherhood was the first place I learned that love could be both armor and undoing. It cracked me open in ways survival never could, forcing me to practice tenderness even when it felt foreign, even when it scared me. And I didn't leave that lesson at home. The mirror Kenzie held up to me followed me into the streets, into the uniform, into every call for service. Even as the badge demanded silence, she demanded honesty. Even as the job asked for armor, she asked for presence.

Motherhood split me open. The badge kept trying to close me back up. And somewhere in that tension, between the softness I was learning and the toughness I was expected to hold, something inside me began to break. The woman who had learned to survive everything suddenly had to learn how to feel again. Kenzie wasn't just my daughter. She was my mirror and my interruption—the undoing that became my remaking. Through her, I learned what it meant to love without condition, to be seen without earning it. But love does not always feel safe, especially when your heart has been trained to brace for impact. Somewhere between wanting to be held and fearing what that would cost, I learned that softness could save me, and still scare me all the same.

CHAPTER 12

When Love Felt Unsafe

*The intimacy that wounded me
before it ever healed*

LOVE NEVER FELT LIKE SAFETY when I was a child. It felt like guessing. I didn't grow up with hugs or casual words of affirmation, the kind that make closeness feel natural. Tenderness was not my first language. Silence had been home. Until love arrived—romantic, messy, and demanding—I didn't know what to do with it. I wanted it. I feared it. I pushed it away, then ached for it back.

In my childhood home, love never reached for me. It handed me chores instead of comfort, silence instead of softness. Affection was measured in responsibilities shouldered and rules obeyed. I learned early that love was conditional, based on performance, behavior, and silence. I remember nights when I longed for someone to notice my tears, only to be handed a list of tasks instead: start the rice, watch your sister, fold the laundry. My body learned shrink when I wanted to be held, to keep moving when I wanted to be still.

Underneath that resistance was something I didn't even recognize then scarcity thinking. When you grow up with food insecurity, everything in life feels transactional. Every choice is calculated. Every relationship is weighed, even without realizing it.

As a child, I learned to read people not by their words, but by their refrigerators. I could clock the difference between kids who brought packed lunches and kids who stood in line with me for the free one. Their sandwiches came with snacks and juice boxes. Mine came with a pinched face, waiting for the lunch lady to stop calling my name loud enough for everyone to hear. My cheeks burned as whispers circled behind me, sneakers squeaking on the cafeteria tile as I carried my tray, heavier with shame than with food. I gravitated toward the kids who had enough to share, not because I understood privilege, but because I understood the security of someone who wouldn't feel the loss.

The habit of measuring worth by what someone could offer followed me into adulthood, shaping the way I loved and the way I left. I didn't just protect my heart—I audited every feeling that came too close. I learned to read people like ledgers, noting who withdrew, who deposited, who left the balance uneven. I measured gestures, silences, apologies, and promises, always tallying what was given and what could be taken away.

When the balance tilted, I adjusted my posture before anyone could notice. I became skilled at pulling back quietly, the kind of leaving that looked like composure but was really fear disguised as control. It felt responsible, almost wise, to know when to step away. But beneath that logic lived something softer—a child's instinct to not be left again.

I told myself I was protecting my peace, but really, I was protecting my wounds. Each exit felt like proof I could still save myself, even when no one was trying to hurt me. I mistook self-preservation for boundaries, mistook guardedness for discernment. And every time I walked away, I convinced myself it was strength, not loneliness, that followed me out the door.

It took years—and therapy, and love that didn't demand performance—to see the truth. What I called independence was often isolation. What I thought was wisdom was really exhaustion. I wasn't building safety; I was maintaining distance. I was still living by the math of scarcity, still believing that love required proof, that worth had to be earned, that safety came from control.

But control can't hold you. It only keeps you company while you hide. I had learned to confuse endurance with devotion, silence with safety, control with care. Love that required nothing of me but honesty felt suspicious. Love that wanted my softness felt dangerous. So even as motherhood cracked me open, fear stitched me shut when it came to intimacy.

Intimacy didn't just scare me in theory, it lived in my body. When someone reached for my hand, my shoulders tensed before my mind could catch up. When a partner brushed my arm in passing, I flinched, as if softness itself were suspicious. My chest tightened when love came too close, like my body was bracing for a blow it couldn't see. And the worst part? I often mistook that tension for safety. I thought guarded meant strong. But in reality, my body was carrying fear where love should have been allowed to rest.

There was a man named Jaxson who saw me, really saw me. The kind who asked about my day and actually waited for the answer. Who noticed when I went quiet and didn't try to fix it—just sat with me in it. He was patient. Consistent. Safe. And I ran from him.

Not all at once. I showed up, I smiled, I let him hold the version of me I thought was "safe enough." But when he reached for more, the tender, unsure, complicated parts, I shut down. I picked fights over nothing. I questioned his intentions. I convinced myself he didn't really mean what he said. I watched for signs he would leave so I could say, See? I knew it.

Even when love was present, loneliness had a way of curling up beside me. I remember lying next to him, heart racing, wishing I could lean into the warmth, into the steady breath that signaled safety. But instead, I held myself still, muscles locked, waiting for him to fall asleep so I could finally release the breath I'd been holding in. The ache of wanting to be close—but choosing distance—was its own kind of heartbreak.

Jaxson didn't storm out. He didn't slam doors or raise his voice. He just grew quieter, the way people do when they've been knocking on the same locked door too long. One night, after another argument I'd picked just to create distance, he sat across from me at the table, his hands folded, eyes tired. "I don't know how to love you if you won't let me," he said. No dramatic exit. No scene. He gathered his things slowly, like he wanted to give me time to stop him. But I didn't. I couldn't. My chest ached, but my lips stayed pressed shut. When the door closed, I laughed under my breath, as if pretending it was a choice I had made would make the hollowness easier to carry. Later, in bed, I stared at the empty side where he used to sleep and whispered, "See? I knew it." But the truth was, I had orchestrated the ending I feared most.

That experience with Jaxson broke something open in me, not just grief, but clarity. It taught me that wanting love and being ready for love are not the same thing. It forced me to confront the ways I had been emotionally unavailable. To see how my independence had turned into isolation. How my strength had become a wall instead of a bridge. It made me ask the hard questions: What would it look like to trust someone with the whole truth of who I am? What would it feel like to stay? And maybe the hardest one: Do I believe I am worthy of love that does not have to be earned?

I am still answering those questions. Still learning how to soften without unraveling, how to stay open even when it feels easier to run.

But I know this now: what I pushed away wasn't just Jaxson, it was a chance. A mirror. A glimpse of what's possible when fear is no longer in charge. Love, I've learned, is not performance. It is not silence. It is not shrinking. Love is presence. Love is truth. Love is the willingness to stay, even when the voice trembles and the arms remember how to flinch. I know now what my younger self could not: real love does not ask you to earn safety or prove your worth. It holds space for your full self, messy, tender, unhealed, and chooses you anyway.

Looking back, I understand that much of my life was spent learning what love wasn't. I learned it wasn't silence. It wasn't performance. It wasn't endurance mistaken for devotion.

I used to think protection meant distance—that silence was safer than the risk of being hurt again. I didn't realize how much work it would take to recondition a heart that had been trained to survive by staying closed. The fortress I built to keep me safe became the same place that kept me lonely. And even now, there are days I still feel its weight pressing against my ribs. But every morning, I make a quiet promise to myself: to reach for peace before control, to choose softness even when it scares me—to remember that safety isn't the absence of fear—it's the presence of trust.

CHAPTER 13

Grief Doesn't Knock

The grief that shattered me before
it showed me how to live

GRIEF DIDN'T KNOCK, but it found its way in anyway. It carved me out, and in the hollow it left behind, I found remnants of love—messy, imperfect, and unfinished. That day changed me. It took something I never thought I could lose: my sense of safety in the uniform, the illusion that control could protect me. The hardest part wasn't the moment itself. It was carrying it home.

After the shooting, I carried the weight in silence. Not because I didn't want to speak, but because I knew what the badge looked like through my family's eyes. To them, police were the danger, not the ones who needed saving. How could I tell them the job had broken something in me too? That I wasn't just a cop with a gun—I was a woman trying to hold herself together after watching innocence die in front of her. At home, I stayed quiet, caught between protecting them from my pain and knowing they might never see past the uniform to the daughter they raised.

Silence became its own kind of armor. I told myself it was strength. But silence has a way of teaching the body to speak in other languages—tight shoulders, clenched jaw, the pulse that never slows. Grief didn't announce itself with sirens or screams; it crept in quietly, like dusk sliding across a room. By all accounts, I should have been happy. I had traveled, seen the world, built a career, raised a beautiful daughter. From the outside, everything looked solid. But inside, something was slipping.

I would sit in my car before a shift, fingers gripping the steering wheel until my palms ached. *Just go in*, I'd whisper. I'd smile when people passed in the hallway, cheeks stiff from the effort. At night, I lay awake staring at the ceiling, body still, mind racing. The smile stayed on. The routine stayed intact. But underneath it all, an ache had settled in, quiet and stubborn.

Kenzie noticed before I ever named it. Children always do. Some nights she'd press her small hands to my cheeks and tilt her head as if studying me.

"Why are you sad, Mommy?" she asked once, voice soft and sure.

"I'm just tired," I told her, and even I didn't believe it.

She climbed into my lap and wrapped her arms around my neck, holding me with a tenderness I hadn't yet learned to give myself. She didn't know it, but she was the first person to teach me how to be held.

Grief doesn't knock. It doesn't wait for a convenient time or the space you've prepared. It just walks in—uninvited, unapologetic, heavy. Sometimes it arrives with a late-night phone call. Sometimes it hides inside four quiet words—*we need to talk*—when you already know what's coming. And sometimes it doesn't announce itself at all; it simply settles in your chest, your bones, the corners of your spirit you thought were safe.

Grief became cumulative. Layer upon layer—death, distance, disappointment—each leaving a fingerprint. Even when I pretended there was no space for it, it found its way in. And through it all, Kenzie was there. She didn't know the details, but she knew the weight. She'd climb into my bed, press her back against my chest, and breathe in sync with me, her way of saying without words: *You're still here. I'm still here.* I needed that reminder, because grief doesn't pause for parenting, and parenting doesn't pause for grief.

It's easy to think grief belongs only to death. But I knew it long before I ever saw a casket. It lived in the quiet after long days when no one asked how I was. It lived in the nights I went to bed aching for a hug that never came. Even then, I was grieving tenderness I had never known. Grief is distance. It's disconnection. It's mourning the mother you wished you had, the father who never fully arrived, the version of yourself you lost trying to survive someone else's chaos. It's the love that didn't last, the friendship that faded, the dream that unraveled slowly without an ending. Some grief wears a date you can circle. Some has no timestamp—just a shadow that follows you from room to room.

For a while, I tried to drink mine away. I had always stayed clear of drugs—I'd seen too many homes destroyed—but alcohol felt acceptable. Normal. Civilized. Until it wasn't. Around my third year as an officer, drinking stopped being celebration and became escape. I wasn't toasting life anymore; I was trying to disappear.

There was so much I hadn't faced: failed relationships, family grief locked behind closed doors, the exhaustion of days filled with death and violence followed by nights pretending I was fine. And there was the abortion—a choice I rarely spoke of but carried like an unmarked grave. I remembered the waiting room where no one held my hand, the drive home with the radio too loud, the way I tucked the memory away as if it had no right to exist. I told myself it was done, over, handled. But my body kept remembering.

We were raised to believe you don't ask for help—you figure it out. No softness. No breaking. Just grind. One night, I came undone in my kitchen. The fridge hummed in the silence. That's when the call came.

My god-sister, incarcerated, struggling, unseen, had taken her own life. Suicide silenced her, but what stayed with me was the silence before it—the pain she must have carried alone, the questions I would never ask. Her silence became a mirror of mine, reflecting every cry for help I'd swallowed. It terrified me to realize that what killed her was the same thing that kept me from reaching out.

My knees buckled. My hands gripped the counter until my knuckles ached. The sobs came from somewhere deep, shaking loose whatever composure I'd built. This wasn't another story I'd heard on the job. This was family. This was laughter I could still hear, a presence I'd assumed would always return. And I couldn't save her.

That night, Kenzie crawled into bed beside me. Her small body, pressed close. She whispered, I love you, Mommy, and drifted to sleep while my tears soaked the pillow. I clung to those words like a life raft, letting them tether me to the living when all I wanted was to sink. In her sleep, she reached for me, fingers curling around my arm as if to make sure I was still there. And in that small gesture, I realized love wasn't asking me to be unbreakable—it was reminding me that I was still here, still worthy of being held.

Not long after, grief struck again. I lost both my grandmother and great-grandmother—pillars of our family, women who had carried histories I never fully knew but always felt. Their presence had been a quiet anchor; their absence, a disorienting void. Losing them felt like losing the ground itself.

I still remember the texture of their hands—soft, wrinkled, steady. My grandmother's house smelled of menthols and fried chicken, grit and comfort intertwined. My great-grandmother never sang. Her silence was its own hymn—strength measured in stillness, love spoken through the work of her hands.

When they left, so much left with them—recipes never written, stories told only in kitchens, lessons passed through gesture instead of word. At their funerals I looked around and realized the keepers of our family memory were gone. The silence they left was louder than any hymn. It settled in my chest—the fear that if I didn't learn to speak, to write, to remember, Kenzie might one day say the same of me.

And the job kept handing me grief I couldn't shake. The sound of a mother screaming when we told her that her teenage son didn't make it—the way her knees gave out, her hands clawing at the air as if she could pull him back by sheer will. That scream followed me home, echoing louder than any siren. Later that night I stood beneath scalding water, pressing my forehead to the tile, tears and steam mingling until I couldn't tell which was which. It was the only place I could unravel unseen, the only space where grief could pour out and circle the drain. But when the water stopped, the ache followed me out.

Grief lived in my body long after words failed. My weight shifted. My stomach knotted until hunger became foreign. Sleep fractured into sweat-soaked fragments. Even on quiet mornings my hands shook reaching for coffee, as if grief had taken residence in my bones.

Yet somewhere inside that unraveling, a flicker of clarity broke through. I began to see grief not only as a thief but as a mirror—showing me what I'd loved enough to lose. Grief, I realized, was love with nowhere to go. As unbearable as it was, it proved I was still capable of feeling, still human enough to hurt.

That truth didn't heal me, but it steadied me. Even in the darkness, I was not beyond hope. Grief is like smoke—it doesn't announce itself; it seeps in slowly, curling into corners until you're choking before you realize it's there. But with time, you learn to open a window, to let the air move again. You start to see that surviving isn't just about enduring the smoke, but remembering light still finds a way through it.

Then came the day that changed everything—the hostage call. Until then, I'd been light on my feet, the officer who smiled, who believed she could protect everyone. But when a man charged with a knife, and shots were fired, innocence slipped from me. He survived. I hadn't fired my weapon. My arms were full—carrying the mother's daughters against my vest as she ran beside me. I had turned my back to danger and chosen to carry life instead. We all lived. But something else died: the belief that the uniform could shield me from breaking.

After that, my smile didn't come as easily. My hand hovered near my gun even in peace. My pulse stayed high, even in silence. One night, after tucking Kenzie in, I snapped at her for leaving the hall light on. She shrank back, eyes wide. Guilt burned instantly. It wasn't the light—it was the fear still living in my chest. That night I learned grief doesn't only wound the one who carries it. It spills onto everyone nearby.

For a long time, I thought grief made me weak. Now I know it makes me honest. Grief isn't something to conquer; it's something to carry with care. When we stop fighting it—when we name it, honor it—it transforms. It becomes less a wound and more a witness, proof that something mattered. I still feel it sometimes: a song, a scent, a flash of memory. I don't run from it anymore. Sometimes I cry. Sometimes I sit quietly. Sometimes I speak to the memory, letting it know it's still held. Grief isn't here to break us. It's here to soften us, to clear what's been blocked, to remind us that even after the pain, love remains.

Some nights I prayed. Other nights I only stared at the ceiling and whispered why. Even in doubt, the asking meant I hadn't given up. Love, even when it aches, is worth carrying. Because grief is proof that love existed. And even now, I carry them with me— my god-sister, whose laughter still echoes; my grandmother and great-grandmother, whose legacies steady me. Their absence is a wound, but their memory is a compass, guiding me back to what matters.

Still, love doesn't erase the fractures it leaves behind. It only teaches you how to live with them—how to trace the cracks without losing the beauty of what remains.

CHAPTER 14

The Cracks Grief Left Behind

The sorrow that settled into my body,
waiting for release

THERE ARE LOSSES THAT CRY out, demanding to be named. And then there are quieter ones—the fractures that leave no obituary, the distance that leaves no gravesite, the versions of ourselves we bury without ceremony. This is the silence of grief, the kind that does not roar but hums beneath the surface, shaping everything and saying nothing.

Quiet grief stripped me bare, but it also gave me room. Room to breathe. Room to laugh. Room to hum again in the car. Even in loss, life insisted on itself. And somehow, so did I.

I remember one birthday evening, sitting on the edge of my bed, my phone heavy in my hand. I refreshed the screen again and again, waiting for a message that never came. With every passing hour, the silence stretched longer. The light from the screen faded across my face, the glow mocking the absence on the other side. It wasn't death I was grieving that night; it was absence—the quiet confirmation that someone who once knew me no longer thought to reach for me.

Not all grief comes with funerals or sirens. Some grief is softer, almost invisible. It slips in through unanswered texts, through birthdays that go unacknowledged, through the ache of being misunderstood by people you once called home. It lingers in the silence after an argument that never found its ending, or in the strange emptiness of hearing your name spoken by someone who no longer knows how to say it with love.

I believed grief belonged only to loss marked by black suits, fried chicken, and church hymns. But I've learned some of the heaviest grief never earns a eulogy. It doesn't arrive with ceremony or comfort. There are no sympathy cards, no white lilies—just an ache that lives in your chest like an unanswered question. A kind of mourning without closure, a loss that lingers in the spaces where words never made it out.

There is grief in watching a relationship with a parent wither, not from a single wound but from years of unopened doors. There is grief in knowing your childhood self never got to be carefree. There is grief in realizing the same survival strategies that carried you this far have become your cage. And there is the grief of a self you had to bury to survive—the girl who laughed loudly, who asked for help without shame, who believed softness didn't make her a target.

That grief does not cry out; it grows quiet. It settles into your jaw, clenched through the day and aching through the night. It hums beneath your headaches, flares in your back, pulses in the numbness you cannot explain. It doesn't always show up as tears. Sometimes it is tightness in your chest. A sudden forgetfulness. A hollow kind of functioning. That was me. I was grieving so many things and didn't even know it: the father who never arrived emotionally, the friendships that slipped into polite distance, the dreams I laid down gently because life made no room. The version of me I lost to "strength."

And grief like that—it collects. It piles up until even joy feels heavy. The good moments come and you don't know how to hold them, because your body is still bracing for disappointment. I remember a Christmas—spades at the card table, music folding through the room, kids tearing open gifts. It should have felt full. But I watched a cousin unwrap a present from his father and saw how easily affection passed between them. That was all it took—a laugh, a hand on a shoulder, simple presence. My father's absence, so routine I thought I'd learned to ignore it, struck me like a fresh wound.

Another time, it was the grocery store that undid me. I turned a corner and froze at the sight of my brother's favorite cereal—Apple Jacks. We used to eat them straight from the box, laughing until our stomachs hurt. My chest tightened. He was alive, but locked behind bars, unreachable.

Sometimes the hardest part wasn't the memories themselves but how easily they surfaced—sudden, ordinary, uninvited. A familiar song, the sound of laughter from another room, or the way light caught in the corner of my eye could undo me. Grief had a way of folding into the everyday, settling between breaths, softening and sharpening all at once. I learned to move carefully around it, as if stillness might keep it from spilling over.

Grief lived in my chest like a stone—thin, heavy, unyielding. My shoulders stayed tense, always bracing for something I couldn't stop. At night, the quiet after the absence was louder than any siren. It followed me into the mornings, settling behind my badge and beneath my smile. I learned how to move through the world while carrying what refused to be put down. There's no ceremony for the kind of loss that blurs family and memory. So I swallowed it. I turned it into endurance. Endurance only sharpened the ache.

And then there were the friendships. No slammed doors, no final words—just the quiet unraveling of something once steady.

Calls grew shorter. Texts slowed, then stopped. Plans dissolved into polite maybes. *We'll circle back*, we said. We didn't. One day I realized I no longer knew the names of their children. The loss never announced itself; it settled in slowly, like dust on a photograph you stopped looking at.

The heaviest grief, though, was for myself—the girl I buried long ago. She sang loud. She cried when the tears came. She laughed without shrinking. She trusted softness was safe. I muted her in the name of survival. Told her she was too much, too tender, too unguarded for this world. Her absence kept pressing against my ribs, asking to be named.

Grief taught me silence. I thought if I named the ache, I'd be dismissed, pitied, told to "be strong." I swallowed it, adding one more layer to the armor I wore every day. But silence doesn't erase grief. It feeds it. It makes the absences echo louder. The more I held it in, the more invisible I became—even to myself.

Sometimes the ache followed me into crowded rooms. One holiday, the house was bright with laughter and music, plates clattering in the kitchen. I smiled when I was supposed to, nodded at the right moments, even laughed on cue. Inside, I felt like a ghost—watching life happen around me while a part of me stood apart, aching for someone to notice.

It swelled until one night the weight broke through, spilling everything I had tried to contain. I was in the shower, steam rising, water scorching hot. I hadn't cried in weeks—maybe months. Not because I didn't want to, but because I had forgotten how. Then, without warning, a sob ripped through me. Not graceful. Not quiet. Guttural. Raw. My knees bent under it. One hand pressed to the tile. My chest heaved, as if I couldn't catch air. It felt like my body was trying to empty decades of silence in a single night.

I cried for everything. For the mother I needed and didn't always have on long nights of self-doubt. For the father whose absence I pretended didn't matter. For the little girl who rode her bike to Safeway with a check she didn't understand, carrying burdens too big for her frame. For the friendships that fell apart when I stopped performing and started telling the truth. For the woman I was before trauma, before the badge, before composure became my mask.

When the sobs finally slowed, I stepped out, dripping, face blotched, eyes swollen. I looked in the mirror and saw myself—raw, undone, real. I wasn't healed. But I was honest. And that, for once, felt like enough.

In the weeks after, grief kept showing up in my body before I had words. Mornings bloomed with a headache no medicine could touch. My back ached in ways that had nothing to do with lifting or long shifts. Some nights I woke at three a.m. with my chest tight, lungs pulling air and never enough—as if I'd been holding my breath in my sleep. My body was grieving long before I gave myself permission to.

Not long after, I sat with my mom at her kitchen table. The refrigerator hummed in the pauses between us, the air heavy with years of unsaid things. She slid a plate toward me—a small square of cornbread, still warm. No speeches. No apologies. Just presence. I let myself take it in—the offering, the nearness, the quiet way she was trying.

I didn't need her to rewrite the past. I needed this moment: her choosing to sit with me, not against me. The grief didn't vanish, but it loosened. I realized what healing sometimes looks like in fractured relationships: not perfection, not explanation—just steady gestures that say I'm here. The words surprised me. They slipped out before I could catch them.

"Sometimes I wish it had been different between us."

I spoke it low, almost ashamed, afraid naming it would break the fragile peace at the table. She didn't rush to answer. She didn't defend herself. She reached across, her hand brushing mine. That small contact said more than any explanation could. In that moment, silence didn't win. I spoke my grief, and it didn't destroy me.

For a long time, I believed if I let myself grieve, I would fall apart and never find my way back. But on the other side of grief, I didn't find destruction. I found tenderness. Not first from others—from myself. And then, sometimes, from unexpected places. A sorority sister noticed when my laugh didn't reach my eyes. She didn't press. She didn't fix. She stayed. Sometimes, staying is what saves. Not all connections fade; some grow stronger in the quiet.

Grief stripped me bare. In the space it left, I began to see something truer: grief is not the opposite of love; it is proof of it. Every ache pointed to someone or something that mattered. Naming it made room for tenderness. Grief did not ruin me the way I feared. It stripped me, yes—left me raw and trembling—but in that rawness I found room. Room to tell the truth without apologizing. Room to imagine a self who wasn't only surviving but deserving of softness.

I began to see grief not as an ending but as a threshold, a doorway between what was and what will never be again. Naming what hurt didn't erase it, but it softened the edges. It gave the ache a shape, a story. I could carry it differently now—less like a hidden wound and more like a scar that speaks of survival. A mark that says: *I was here. I loved. I lost. I am still living.*

Outside me, not much changed. The bills still stacked. The badge still weighed what it weighed. The silences in my family didn't suddenly dissolve. But inside, something shifted. I breathed deeper. I laughed once—loud and unguarded—and didn't swallow it back. I caught myself humming in the car, the way I hadn't since I was a girl. Small things, almost unremarkable. Signs, all the same. Proof that even in loss, a part of me was still reaching for life.

And then there was Kenzie. One night she climbed onto the couch beside me, curls damp from the bath, the smell of cocoa butter warm on her skin. She leaned into me without asking, a simple weight against my side.

"You look tired, Mom," she said, and wrapped her arms around me as if her small body could anchor mine. I laughed, surprised by the tenderness, and—for once—I didn't brush it off. I let her hold me. Later her laughter rang through the house like a bell. She became the clearest proof that I was still capable of more than survival. In her small hands, I saw reflections of myself, parts I thought grief had swallowed, parts I wasn't sure how to hold.

Now I know this: silence no longer means I am disappearing. Sometimes silence means I am breathing. Sometimes it means I am choosing presence over performance. Sometimes it means I am still here—alive, grounded, with enough room to hold grief and love at once. If grief taught me anything, it's that even in stillness, survival takes strength.

But survival has a cost. I wore composure like armor, convinced being fine was the same as being okay. It took me years to learn the difference—years to notice how light finds its way through what's cracked, not what's flawless. The cracks grief left behind did not close. They became windows. And I am learning to live with the light.

CHAPTER 15

The Weight of Being Fine

*The cost of pretending
I was unshaken and unbroken*

THE MIRROR SAID I WAS FINE, uniform pressed, hair freshly braided back into two cornrows, a smile rehearsed to match the neatness. Everything in its place, even as nothing inside me was fine. "Morning, Saunders," an officer called as I passed through the hallway. I nodded, shoulders squared, the word fine already loaded on my tongue like muscle memory.

"You good?"

"Yeah," I said. "I'm fine."

But my chest was tight, lungs rationing each breath. My temples throbbed like a warning siren only I could hear. The taste of last night's whiskey still clung to the back of my throat. Inside, I was unraveling. Outside, I was flawless.

That's the thing about "fine." It doesn't ask questions or invite truth. It's both shield and shackle, the word that keeps everyone else comfortable while making me disappear. I wore it until it nearly killed me. Fine almost finished me. But truth, spoken out loud, whispered in therapy, held in my daughter's small hands, is what saved me. I am still here. And that is its own kind of miracle.

"I'm fine." I said it so often it became muscle memory, a reflex that rolled off my tongue before anyone could look too closely. Fine was my camouflage, my fortress, my shield. But behind those two words lived exhaustion, loneliness, and a darkness I didn't dare name. It didn't happen in one moment, it was the accumulation of years. Grief stacked on silence. Silence stacked on duty. Duty stacked on a smile I wore like armor. By the time I realized how heavy it all was, I had already convinced everyone, including myself, that I was fine.

Fine nearly buried me. It's only four letters, soft and simple, the kind of word that slides easily past the lips. It doesn't demand anything of the one who hears it, and it doesn't reveal anything about the one who says it. But for me, fine was heavy. Fine suffocated me. Fine became the mask that almost became my coffin. The danger of "fine" is that it passes as harmless. It looks steady enough to be strength, warm enough to feel believable, detached enough to end a conversation before it even starts. I learned to wield "fine" like a shield. And one night, that shield nearly killed me.

"Hey sis, how are you really doing?" The question floated across the table, her voice raised just enough to cut through the buzz of happy hour. Ice clinked in glasses. Laughter burst from the next booth. Bass thumped low from the playlist overhead. The smell of fried food clung to the air, salt and grease mixing with the sharp tang of lemon in her drink.

We'd been trying for weeks to align our schedules, and finally here we were, two women unwinding after long days, drinks in hand, appetizers on the way. It should have been the perfect moment to exhale. But I didn't. Instead, I slipped into my role. Smiled. Tilted my head just so. Reached for my script.

"I'm fine." The words came out smooth, polished from years of practice. And just like always, they worked. She nodded, accepted the answer, and steered the conversation elsewhere. We laughed about work, traded gossip, stole fries off each other's plates, and clinked glasses when the punchline landed. From the outside, it looked like two friends catching up after too long apart.

But inside, my chest was a clenched fist. Every laugh cracked something brittle in me. Every smile felt like an act. That's the trap of fine, it doesn't just cover the cracks, it deepens them. Every time I said it, I paid. My silence bought everyone else comfort, but it cost me pieces of myself I didn't know how to get back. And the more I played the part, the harder it became to tell the truth.

At work, fine wasn't just habit, it was policy. Roll call buzzed with the shuffle of boots, the squawk of radios, the sharp smell of burnt coffee clinging to the cinderblock walls. Someone cracked a joke, and the room erupted. Laughter ricocheted around us, sharp and sudden, pressing in like static.

I joined in, loud enough to blend. My lips pulled into a smile, my shoulders shook with practiced ease. But under the table, my hands trembled so hard I pressed them flat against my thighs. My jaw locked until it ached. My stomach knotted into something immovable. A supervisor passed behind me, clapped my shoulder. "How you holding up?" His tone was casual, almost rhetorical. I smiled. Nodded. Said the line.

"I'm fine." He believed me. They all did. When roll call ended, I walked out with my head high, my boots steady, my uniform sharp. The perfect picture of composure. But the minute I sat in my patrol car, the performance collapsed. The echoes of laughter clanged in my head until they turned hollow. I gripped the steering wheel, chest tight, lungs straining. My vision blurred, not from tears but from the migraine pounding behind my eyes. For a few terrifying minutes I sat completely still, unsure if I would ever draw a full breath again.

Then the tears came. Hot. Fast. Unrelenting. They soaked into my uniform, dampened the radio cord, streaked down my face until I slumped forward against the cold steering wheel, its ridges pressed against my forehead. The silence afterward was heavier than the noise. And in that quiet, the sharpest truth hit: if I disappeared tomorrow, that room would keep buzzing. The laughter would return. And someone would say, *but she said she was fine.*

There were nights I drove aimlessly through the city, windows down, music blasting rattling the doors. I gripped the wheel until my fingers cramped, the streetlights smearing into streaks of yellow. Portland passed in fragments—bridges arching over the Willamette, neon signs buzzing against wet pavement, couples walking hand in hand on sidewalks slick with rain I no longer felt of. I sang along too loudly, off-key and desperate, trying to drown the silence in my head. But no matter how high I turned the volume, the silence underneath always won.

Sometimes I drove through the neighborhoods where I grew up, past corners that looked the same but felt foreign. The streets that once held childhood games now held shadows of who I used to be. The fading murals, the hum of streetlights—they all whispered of a life I had outgrown but never fully left behind. And somewhere between those streets and the stillness that followed, I realized how lonely survival could feel.

I told myself I was just clearing my head, but really, I was circling. Stalling. Outrunning the weight that always found me again when I pulled into my driveway. Those drives weren't about getting somewhere; they were about avoiding the place where silence waited, patient as ever.

The night it nearly ended was unremarkable in every way. The house was quiet. Too quiet. The refrigerator buzzed. The clock ticked. Shadows stretched long across the wall, broken only by the faint hum of the streetlight outside my window. Everything looked ordinary, and that was the most terrifying part, how my ending could come wrapped in stillness.

I had a plan. Clean. Precise. No drama. No mess. I told myself that was responsible, as if an ending could ever be tidy. And the calm of it, that was what scared me most. My phone sat on the table, its glow casting shadows across my hands. I thought about picking it up. I thought about how exhausting explaining myself would be. The silence thickened.

I imagined the aftermath, my daughter at someone else's kitchen table, repeating the same script I had inherited. *I'm fine.* I imagined coworkers shaking their heads at roll call. I imagined the whispers, the judgment, the headline. And, I sat there, rehearsing my exit.

What saved me wasn't bravery or clarity–it was inconvenience. I texted my daughter's father, asked if he could keep her for a few days. I told him I wasn't feeling well, that I needed rest. What I couldn't say was: If he picked her up, I knew I wouldn't survive the night. His reply came fast. *Can't. Maybe in a few weeks.*

The words landed like stones in my chest. My perfect, quiet plan unraveled in an instant. Rage surged first, at him, at myself, at the universe for refusing to let me go quietly. My hand shook so hard I nearly dropped the phone. I wanted to smash it against the wall, to hear something else break besides me. Then the rage gave way.

A sob ripped out of me, violent and unexpected. Proof that some part of me still wanted to live. Proof that the calm wasn't the whole story. In that crack, my daughter's presence filled the silence. If I left, she would inherit the same script that nearly destroyed me. I couldn't let "fine" become her inheritance. So, I stayed.

Weeks later, I finally told the truth in therapy. It was harder than I expected. I sat on the edge of the couch, hands twisting in my lap, throat raw from silence, eyes fixed on the yellow legal pad waiting like it already knew my secrets. My therapist waited. She didn't push. Didn't rush. Just sat there, steady, while I wrestled with the weight of it. Finally, the words broke loose.

"I almost ended it."

The room was still. My chest heaved like I'd run a mile. Tears blurred my vision. I braced for judgment, for shock, for disappointment. Instead, she nodded softly. "You're here," she said. "And that matters." I had built a life on holding everything in, and here I was, spilling the truth in a room that didn't collapse under it. I sobbed harder, but it wasn't despair, it was relief. Relief that I wasn't carrying it alone anymore.

For so long, I thought strength meant never breaking. I thought survival meant holding it all together no matter the cost. I know now: silence doesn't save you, it suffocates you. The bravest thing you can do is break the script. Say what terrifies you. Let yourself be seen.

"I'm fine" nearly cost me my life. Now I say something truer: I'm hurting. I'm healing. I'm here. Strength is the expectation for Black women, but it's also the silence that kills us. We are praised for holding it together, but rarely given permission to fall apart. I am learning to give that permission to myself.

If you are the strong one, the fun one, the one who looks like they have it all together, hear me: it is okay to break. It is okay to need. It is okay to ask. And for the rest of us, the friends, the coworkers, the family, don't settle for the easy answer. Don't take fine at face value. Ask again. Press gently but firmly. Sometimes what saves a life isn't a grand rescue. Sometimes it is a minute of presence. A voice that says, *I see you. I care.*

That night became my line in the sand. I could no longer pretend that "fine" was enough. Therapy didn't fix me overnight. My

121

daughter's love didn't erase the darkness. But speaking the truth, first in a whisper, then in a steady voice, gave the pain somewhere to go besides inward. It gave me a map back to myself.

I started small. One honest text instead of an automatic smiley face. One "I'm tired" instead of "I'm fine." One moment of sitting with my daughter and letting her see me cry. Each time, the world didn't end. The sky didn't fall. In fact, something softer opened between me and the people I trusted. The more I named what hurt, the less power it had over me.

It's still uncomfortable sometimes. Some days the old reflex rises, and "I'm fine" hovers on my tongue, familiar as breath. But now I know it costs. I know that silence doesn't make me strong—it only makes me smaller, harder to find. For so long, disappearing felt like safety. Now, I want to be seen. I want to stay.

I want to be here. For my daughter. For myself. For every Black woman who has been told that strength is her only option. For everyone who has ever swallowed their own despair so no one else would feel uncomfortable. If you are reading this and you are wearing "fine" like armor, I hope my story reaches you. I hope you let one person see you. I hope you speak one hard truth out loud. You deserve to stay. You deserve to breathe. You deserve to live beyond survival.

I am still learning to live beyond survival. Still learning that I don't have to hold it all. Still learning that the bravest thing I can say isn't "I'm fine," but "I'm here." "Fine" almost finished me. Truth saved me. Staying saved me. Love is still saving me. And sometimes, when I catch my reflection in the mirror, I pause—not to check my hair or my uniform, but to whisper to the woman staring back at me: You're here. And that matters.

Somewhere along the way, I began to understand that strength doesn't always sound like silence or look like composure. Sometimes it shows up in softness—in the trembling voice that still chooses to speak, in the heart that stays open after breaking. That's where healing began–and where softness became strength.

PART IV

When Softness Became Strength

*The cracks in my armor, the risk of being
touched, the courage of letting go.*

Strength once meant surviving without softness.
But survival is not the same as living.

Softness waited for me in places I was
afraid to stay, asking me to risk joy,
to risk trust, to risk being held.

CHAPTER 16

The Risk of Being Held

*The safety that sometimes looked
like staying in open arms*

I DID NOT GROW UP WITH SOFTNESS. Not the kind you see in movies, the warm embraces, the gentle affirmations, the freedom to fall apart and still be held. I grew up with resilience. With strength. With "you'll be alright" and "fix your face." Love was present, yes, but it was practical. Provision, not presence. Direction, not dialogue. We didn't say, "I'm proud of you." We handed you a plate. We didn't ask, "How do you feel?" We asked, "What's next?"

I remember one afternoon as a little girl, running into the house after being shoved at school. My knees were scraped, gravel still clinging to my skin, tears burning as they spilled down my face. What I wanted was someone to scoop me up, to brush away the dirt, to say the words every child longs for: you're safe now, I've got you. Instead, I was met with a sigh and a sharp command: "Stop crying, fix your face."

The sting on my knees was nothing compared to the sting in my chest. That day, I learned tears were trouble. That needing comfort made me weak. That silence and toughness were the only coverings strong enough to survive. And so I swallowed my cries. Again and again. Until my body forgot what it felt like to fall apart in someone's arms.

By adulthood, silence had settled into my bones. I didn't know how to cry without apologizing. I didn't know how to lean without fearing the weight would break the person beneath me. I didn't know how to be held. When softness found its way into my life, through therapy, through my daughter's little hands cupping my face, through the quiet kindness of people who loved me without needing me to perform, I didn't know how to receive it. I flinched. I questioned it. I braced for the catch. Because when you have lived your whole life armored, even kindness feels dangerous. Even love feels like a setup.

Then came a man who was steady. Kind. Soft in a way I wasn't used to. He didn't try to fix me or lecture me out of my feelings. He simply listened. Waited. Stayed close. His presence should have felt like safety. Instead, it felt like exposure. One night, a small trigger unraveled me. Tears clogged my throat, my chest cinched like I was drowning on dry land. My body went rigid as panic rushed in: Don't show too much. Don't scare him away. Don't let him see the wreck under the surface. I scrambled for distance, blurting apologies I couldn't stop. "I'm sorry. I'm too much. You deserve better. Just go before I ruin this." He didn't argue. He didn't move away. He just pulled me into his arms, slow and deliberate, like he was approaching a wounded animal.

"You don't have to fight me," he whispered. But my body didn't believe him. My shoulders locked, my fists clenched, my heartbeat pounded like a warning drum. Every cell rehearsed betrayal before it even arrived. That's what survival had carved into me: don't trust comfort, don't rely on care, don't believe safety is real. I had mastered pain. I hadn't learned how to accept peace. Even as he stayed, I pulled away. Not in one loud break, but in a hundred tiny retreats. Missed calls. Short answers. A laugh that didn't reach my eyes. Slowly, silently, I left. When it ended, there was no explosion. Just silence. And then the shame.

Shame came at night. It came in the hollow hours after midnight, when the house was still and my mind replayed everything I didn't say. I would lie awake staring at the ceiling, phone in my hand, fighting the urge to text him: I'm sorry. I didn't mean it. Please come back. My body ached with words I couldn't release. I told myself I had done the right thing, that I had protected myself. But deep down, I knew: I hadn't protected myself. I protected my fear. Survival has a way of justifying itself in the dark. Better alone. Better armored. Better unseen. That's what I told myself as I lay rigid in bed, rehearsing the script I had inherited. Because the truth is, my fear wasn't born with me. It was modeled for me.

I thought of my grandmother, her back straight, her grief unspoken, her tears always held just behind her eyes. I thought of my mother, always composed, always busy, never once collapsing in front of us. Their strength kept us alive, but it also handed me a script: silence was noble, needing was weakness, and the safest way to love was to keep it contained. That script had built me, and it was the very thing I was now trying to unlearn.

Softness kept finding me, though. It didn't always come dressed as romance. Sometimes it showed up in friendship—steady and unspoken. Sometimes it came through my daughter, in the way she reached for me without hesitation. And sometimes it arrived in the quiet moments when I had to choose between running and staying, between the comfort of distance and the risk of being seen.

One evening, I sat on the edge of my bed with my head in my hands, trying to cry quietly so my daughter wouldn't hear. But kids always know. She padded into the room in her pajamas, hair wild from sleep, and climbed onto my lap. Without asking, she pressed her palms to my cheeks, tilted my face up, and whispered, "It's okay, Mommy. You can cry." The words split something inside me. No one had ever said that to me before. Not once had my tears been welcomed, let alone affirmed. I wanted to swallow them back, to protect her from my sadness, but her little hands held me steady. And in her eyes I saw the truth: softness was possible, and it could begin again with us. That night, I didn't run. I didn't apologize. I let my tears fall into her hands, and I let myself be held. But learning softness was never a straight line.

There was another night, later, when the weight of it all pressed so heavily I found myself pacing the kitchen. Dishes in the sink, the hum of the refrigerator, the house dark except for one light over the stove. My chest was tight, my throat raw from holding back tears. A friend sat across from me, waiting. She had come over after hearing the strain in my voice on the phone.

I wanted to collapse, but my body screamed to run. My hand hovered near the counter's edge as if bracing for escape. My mouth filled with apologies before the tears even fell. "I shouldn't do this. I'm sorry. I don't know why I can't just get it together. I don't want to be a burden." Every instinct told me to pull away. To wipe my face. To make a joke. To retreat into silence. I could almost feel the doorframe calling me, an exit from the exposure of being seen. But she didn't let me retreat. She crossed the kitchen, slow but steady, and placed both her hands on my shoulders. "Breathe," she said, voice low and unwavering. "Stay here."

I froze. The fight in me flared, muscles tight, jaw clenched, eyes darting like a trapped animal. Then came the trembling, a quake starting in my chest and spilling down my arms. My body shook with the effort of not running. And then something cracked. A sob ripped through me, so loud it startled me. I collapsed against her shoulder, the sound of my own crying foreign and jagged. My fists

130

unclenched. My knees bent. My whole weight leaned into her. I expected her to let go, to step back, to tell me it was too much. But she didn't move. She held me, firm and steady, as though my shaking body wasn't a burden but a body worth carrying.

In that kitchen, under the dim light, I experienced something new: the terror of surrender meeting the relief of being caught. For once, I stayed. And in staying, I realized something generational was shifting. My grandmother never collapsed in front of anyone. My mother never showed her tears. But I, right there in that kitchen, was breaking the script. My daughter would not only inherit strength from me; she would inherit softness too.

It wasn't only lovers or my daughter who taught me softness. It was friends who refused to let me disappear, who held space for the parts of me I once hid. It was therapists teaching me how to breathe through panic instead of bolt from it, how to trust that stillness wouldn't break me. And it was my own body—trembling but staying—finally learning what it meant to unclench, to surrender without losing itself.

Months later, long after the breakup, I woke up in the middle of the night gasping for air. A nightmare had shaken me awake. A gun. A flash. Bodies I could not save. The kind of memory policing had etched into my nervous system. My instinct was to spring up, to pace the room, to swallow it down before anyone saw. That was what I always did.

But that night my daughter stirred beside me. Half-asleep, she draped her arm over my waist. My first impulse was to slip out from under it, to get up and be "strong" somewhere alone. Instead, something in me paused. Her small arm anchored me, reminding me of the night she told me it was okay to cry. I stayed. My body screamed to flee, but I stayed.

Her breath warmed my shoulder, steady and unbothered, as if she already knew the truth I was still learning: I did not have to be afraid of being held. In that stillness I realized that courage was not the absence of fear. Courage was unclenching my fists, sinking into the mattress, and allowing presence, no matter how small, to hold me through the night.

Softness terrified me because it meant surrender. And surrender had never felt safe, especially for Black women. We are praised for being unbreakable, for carrying generations on our backs, for doing it all flawlessly and thanklessly. We are admired for our hustle and our silence. But where is the celebration for our rest? Our tears? Our tenderness?

It took years of therapy to unlearn the lie that strength meant never needing anything. For so long, I thought independence was armor, that needing help made me weak. But healing asked me to relearn everything I thought I knew—to see that true strength makes space for rest, that it looks like honesty, that it sounds like asking for help, that it feels like choosing softness without shame. The kind of strength that doesn't demand perfection, only presence. The kind that lets you lay your armor down and still know you're safe.

Unlearning had to start with my body, because my body had memorized danger. In therapy, my counselor taught me a simple practice that felt ridiculous at first: thirty seconds of stillness with my hand over my heart. "Let your hand be a weight that says 'stay,'" she said. "Notice what tries to run." The first week, my leg bounced like it had a life of its own. My jaw clenched. My breath stayed shallow, as if deeper breathing might invite grief I couldn't control. But I kept trying. Breath in for four, out for six. Feet on the floor. Name five things I could see, four I could feel, three I could hear. The exercises didn't fix me; they helped me hear myself. I learned the difference between the ache of old fear and the ache of being human. I learned that "I'm overwhelmed" was not a failure, but a north star pointing me toward care.

Tenderness met me in unglamorous places too. A nurse once wrapped my ankle after surgery and said, "You don't have to be brave with me." The room smelled like antiseptic, the fluorescent lights were harsh, and yet her words softened something the pain meds couldn't touch. I remember nodding and then, embarrassingly, tearing up as she adjusted the brace with such care it felt like a blessing. It was small. It was ordinary. It was everything. Sometimes the body believes kindness before the mind does.

There were setbacks, because unlearning rarely moves in straight lines. One afternoon, a friend texted, "Proud of you. You're doing beautifully." I stared at the screen, suspicious of a compliment meant for me. My thumb hovered over a deflection: *It's nothing.* Instead, I tried a new sentence that tasted like a foreign language: "Thank you. That means a lot." I put the phone down and sat with the urge to take it back. My cheeks burned. My chest tightened. Nothing exploded. The world did not end because I let goodness land. That tiny acceptance felt like a seed.

Another time, softness came dressed as repair. I snapped at someone I loved—tired, hungry, triggered. The old script said disappear, pretend it didn't happen, or bury myself in shame. Softness asked for something braver: I circled back. "I'm sorry," I said, voice low. "I was flooded. I care about you. Can we try again?" They nodded, eyes kind. We reset the conversation. I learned that being held doesn't always mean arms around you; sometimes it means being trusted enough to repair what your fear cracked.

And then there was the day I attempted rest on purpose. No emergency. No meltdown. Just a Saturday with sun pouring across the living room floor. I made tea, turned my phone face down, and laid on the rug beside my daughter. We read different books in the same quiet. At first my brain sputtered with to-do lists, reasons to get up, reasons I hadn't earned this. Then the minutes stretched, slow and generous. The tenderness was so plain it almost disguised itself as nothing. But I felt it—certainty settling in my bones like warm light: this is allowed.

Softness is not weakness. It is a reclamation. A declaration that I deserve to be loved, not for what I do, but for who I am. And somewhere in that unlearning, something unexpected bloomed alongside the grief: joy.

At first, joy startled me. It felt fragile—like a bubble I wasn't supposed to touch. Even in laughter, I caught myself bracing, waiting for the other shoe to drop. Happiness made me uneasy, because joy meant I had something to lose. Sometimes I tried to outrun it, to push it away before it could disappear on its own. It took time to understand that joy was never asking me to trust its permanence—only to let it exist, even if just for a moment.

Slowly, I learned to stay. To laugh without apology. To dance barefoot in the kitchen. To let rest settle into my bones without rushing to earn it. I think of one evening, music playing low, my daughter and I twirling barefoot across the kitchen tiles, both of us laughing so hard our sides ached. There was no performance. No armor. No script. Just joy. For once, I didn't brace for it to end. I let it wash over me like proof that softness doesn't always lead to loss. Sometimes it leads to freedom.

Joy stopped being a stranger and started to feel like home. The more I let myself taste it, the more I understood that joy—like softness—is not fragile. It is a rebellion. A quiet refusal to let survival have the last word. Joy is the bravest kind of endurance—not the kind that hardens, but the kind that opens, again and again, even after everything tried to close you.

Now I know this: there is strength in saying, "I'm not okay." There is strength in being held when every part of you wants to run. There is strength in trusting joy enough to let it soften the edges of a life built on survival. Because love is not a trap. Love is a bridge. It requires courage to cross, yes, but the view on the other side is connection, healing, freedom. And maybe that is what softness has been asking of me all along. Not just to let love in, but to have the courage to be held.

When I think of my grandmother's silence, my mother's stoicism, and my own years of hiding, I realize softness is not only my rebellion. It is my offering back to them. They gave me strength that kept me alive. Now I am adding tenderness that lets me live. Softness is not what undoes me. It is what remakes me. When I let myself be held by my daughter's small arms, by a friend's refusal to let me shrink, by a nurse's steady hands, by a compliment I decide to believe, by laughter echoing through a kitchen, I am rewriting the script I inherited.

Joy doesn't erase their strength; it expands it. Maybe that's the truest kind of courage—not to keep fighting, but to finally let yourself be caught. To stop running from what wants to hold you. To let love, softness, and rest do the saving for once.

CHAPTER 17

Learning to Trust Joy

*The belief that happiness could remain
and not vanish overnight*

THERE WAS A TIME WHEN JOY FELT DANGEROUS, too light, too fleeting, too easy to lose. I had learned how to brace for the blow— to tighten my body like a fist before the hit, to scan every room for exits and every person for threats. I anticipated the fallout before the fall; I prepared for pain so thoroughly that when it came, it felt familiar, even expected. But no one ever taught me how to prepare for joy.

No one told me that receiving good things could make your chest tighten just the same—that peace, when you have lived without it, can feel like walking across glass: careful, cautious, afraid it might shatter beneath your feet. I did not know how to soften into safety or how to hold happiness without scanning the horizon for the next storm. I had spent so long surviving the worst that I did not know what to do when something good stayed. No one told me that peace could be just as fragile, just as sacred, and sometimes even harder to trust.

I remember the first time I laughed—really laughed—after my grandmother died. It was not the polite kind that makes others comfortable around your grief, but a full-bodied, unexpected laugh that escaped before I could stop it. I was at a barbecue with family. The sun was out, music playing low. Someone told a ridiculous story—something so absurd it cracked the heavy shell I had been living inside since the funeral. I do not remember the story, but I remember the way laughter rose out of me, uninvited. I laughed until my stomach hurt, until my eyes watered. For a second, I felt light. Free.

It was like coming up for air after being underwater for too long. A flicker of joy reminded me that I was still alive, still capable of feeling something other than sorrow. But then came the guilt. Joy felt like something I had to apologize for, like laughing meant I was forgetting her, betraying the weight of my love.

For the rest of that afternoon, I watched the light shift across the yard as if testing whether it would stay. The sun moved slowly—steady, indifferent to my guilt. Kids ran past with dripping popsicles, music floated through the air, and the smell of charcoal clung to my clothes. I remember thinking how unfair it was that the world could keep spinning while I was still learning how to breathe inside it.

Grief makes everything feel too sharp—the laughter of others, the color of the sky, even the sweetness of lemonade. I sat there trying to decide if it was okay to feel both broken and grateful at the same time. The truth was, I didn't yet trust my joy to stay put. It felt borrowed, like the universe might change its mind and take it back if I got too comfortable. So I laughed carefully, as if moderation could save me from loss.

Grief is strange like that. It doesn't just take from you—it makes you question the moments you get back. The laughter feels borrowed, and the joy feels suspicious. But maybe laughter is not the absence of grief; maybe it is proof that love still lives in you—that healing has begun, however slowly.

Later that night, I sat in my car and cried—not just for the loss, but for something I had not expected: the unfamiliarity of joy. The way it startled me. The way it felt foreign, like a language I had not spoken in years. I cried because joy no longer felt like home. It felt risky, like something I had to take in small doses, as if I didn't deserve to feel it fully anymore.

Grief had built a wall around me, and I had mistaken it for shelter. I had learned how to survive the storm, but not how to welcome the sun. Joy had become unsafe, as if it might vanish if I reached for it too eagerly. I sat there in the dark—headlights off, engine humming—and cried for the parts of me that did not know how to receive what was beautiful, for the parts that feared peace more than pain. And in that stillness, I whispered what I had not said in a long time: *It is okay to feel this too.*

Even if it doesn't stay. Even if it scares me. Even if my grief still rides in the passenger seat. That moment taught me something I had never known—joy doesn't erase grief; it lives beside it. It breathes beside it. And somehow, that makes the living possible.

At times joy shows up quietly—in the first sip of coffee before the world stirs, in a song that makes you dance before your mind catches up, in the soft laugh of someone you love. These are not distractions from pain; they are tiny rebellions, reminders that say, I'm still here. I'm still choosing life.

For a long time, I thought joy was a luxury, something earned only after the healing was done. But joy is part of healing. It is proof that the darkness did not win. Trusting joy takes practice. It means trusting yourself to survive whatever comes next. It means letting the moment be the moment, imperfect, surprising, alive.

There are still days when joy scares me, when it feels like a setup. But more often now, I let it land. I let it bloom. And when it does,

I hold it close, not like a secret but like a promise. A promise that there is more to life than pain. That there is more to me than what I have survived. That I was made for joy too.

And yet, even with joy growing in small and sacred ways, another truth lingers. You can have a full schedule, a full house, even a full heart, and still feel empty. Loneliness does not always look how we expect. In quiet hours it hides in the silence after a laugh, in the unanswered text message, in the scroll through your contacts wondering who you can be real with.

Sometimes it comes at night, after the mask has slipped, after the job is done, and you feel invisible. I would come home to a quiet house after a long shift, drop my keys on the counter, peel off the uniform that had become a second skin, and move through the house like a ghost—body present, spirit elsewhere.

It was not the kind of loneliness that comes from being alone, but the kind that lingers even when you are surrounded by people. I spent my days shoulder to shoulder with coworkers, solving problems, saving face. But still, I felt unseen. Known for what I did, not for who I was. Joy felt like a language I was still learning to pronounce—but loneliness, loneliness was fluent. I could speak it without effort.

And yet, in the same breath, something inside me kept whispering that there had to be more. That life couldn't just be made of resilience and exhaustion. At times I would catch my reflection in the window, tired eyes still searching, and I would whisper a small prayer: teach me how to stay soft here. It wasn't dramatic, just quiet hope. The kind that keeps you reaching for light even when you don't know if morning will come.

And the truth? I didn't want to reach out. Not because I didn't crave connection, but because vulnerability had begun to feel like a risk I couldn't afford. I didn't want to seem too needy, too emotional, too much. I stayed quiet. Scrolled my phone. Ate in silence. Told myself I was fine. But strength without connection becomes a cage.

Even the strongest person longs to be held, if not by arms, then by understanding. I was carrying the world in a heart that did not know how to ask for help. That kind of silence does not just echo, it erodes. I wanted someone to ask how I was doing and stay long enough to hear the real answer, but I was afraid to ask. Too afraid to be disappointed.

That is when I realized the loneliest place is not being alone, it is being loved only in fragments. Being celebrated for what you do, but unseen for who you are. I used to wear independence like a badge of honor—I do not need anyone, I told myself. I was capable, resilient, and resourceful. Achingly, profoundly lonely. Because independence without intimacy is just isolation in a prettier outfit.

I built walls so carefully that I started believing they were windows. I could see people, smile, and function, but no one could really come in. And when I did try, when I let someone close, it felt like losing control. So I ghosted. Withdrew. Sabotaged. Not because I did not care, but because I cared too much and did not trust myself to survive if they left.

That is the lonely place, the space between wanting and fearing connection, between craving closeness and being terrified of what it might cost. There were days when I wanted company just to feel like I existed. Sometimes I wished someone would check on me the way I checked on others. In certain moments strength felt like a prison I built with my own hands.

Real strength isn't in armor—it's in unmasking. It's saying, I miss you, even if your voice shakes. It's letting people see the human beneath the polished. Connection doesn't require perfection; it just asks for presence, honesty, small, brave moments of openness.

I am learning that I am not broken for feeling lonely. I am just human. So I make space for small openings. Not grand gestures, just simple moments: a truthful conversation over coffee, a shared silence that does not feel heavy, a text that says, I am thinking of you, even when my instinct is to retreat.

Intimacy does not always arrive loudly. Sometimes it whispers through eye contact that lingers, through someone remembering your favorite song, through a question asked with genuine care. These are sacred offerings, invitations to step out of armor and into connection.

I still retreat sometimes. I still go quiet. But now I notice it. I do not stay hidden as long. I'm practicing the return—the return to people, to presence, to myself. And in that return, I am learning what it means to belong. Not because I have mastered vulnerability, but because I have decided connection is worth the risk. Being known, even a little, is better than living behind walls.

Belonging is not about perfection. It is about choosing, over and over, to show up anyway. To let someone reach for you. To reach back. To believe that closeness does not threaten independence, it softens it. Strengthens it. Reminds you that you were never meant to carry everything alone. Because joy and loneliness are not opposites. They coexist. Some of the most joyful moments carry an undercurrent of longing, and some of the loneliest nights hold unexpected beauty—the way moonlight touches a wall, or how music can make your chest ache in the best possible way.

Joy and loneliness both speak to the same truth: *I want to feel.* To be fully alive. To be seen beyond the roles I play. To laugh without bracing for loss. To cry without shame. To be vulnerable without fearing I will be too much or not enough. So no, joy and loneliness are not contradictions. They are companions, evidence of a heart still beating, still willing. And I am learning to honor both. To hold space for the ache and the light. To let my heart stretch wide enough to carry it all. Because now I believe I deserve all of it.

Joy has taught me to stay present, even when the ache lingers nearby. It reminds me that I do not have to wait until everything is healed to feel something good. But it also reveals this truth: even the brightest moments can feel lonely when lived in isolation. Because after we learn to soften, after we learn to trust joy, comes the most vulnerable step of all, letting others witness us in that softness. Belonging is not just about being seen. It is about allowing ourselves to be known. And that kind of intimacy, the kind where you risk being fully yourself in front of someone else, that is where real connection lives. And that is exactly where I was headed next.

Joy shattered something open in me, but it also revealed what still needed tending. I could feel how often I still dimmed myself to keep others comfortable, how I folded my edges just to fit inside someone else's expectations. Healing taught me how to feel, but the next lesson would teach me how to expand. It was time to unlearn the smallness I once mistook for safety.

CHAPTER 18

Unlearning Smallness

The lie that shrinking myself was the only way to survive

I CAN'T REMEMBER THE EXACT AGE, only how it felt to be too much. On picture day, I wore my favorite outfit, bright colors, bold patterns, and clothes that made me feel alive. When the photographer lifted his camera, I smiled wide, unafraid to be seen. Later that day, a classmate wrinkled her nose and said, "You're so extra... even in your clothes." Everyone laughed, and I laughed too, though my chest tightened. The next year, I chose something plain. No bold colors, no wide smile. I wanted to disappear just enough to avoid the sting of being "too much."

That moment followed me like a quiet shadow. I learned to make myself smaller in ways that went far beyond clothes.. I softened my voice, measured my tone, and studied what made people comfortable so I could fit inside it. When I joined law enforcement—the shrinking took on a different shape. The uniform became both armor and permission—a way to take up space without question, as long as I stayed within its boundaries. Outside of it, I found myself shrinking again, afraid to be seen in full color, full voice, full emotion. Even in relationships, I learned to tuck away the parts of me that felt too loud, too opinionated, too tender. Somewhere along the way, I started confusing humility with invisibility: mistaking silence for peace.

It didn't take long for the message to repeat itself in other places. At school, when I raised my hand too often, a teacher said, "Let's give someone else a turn. You don't have to answer every question." At home, if I cried too loudly, I was told, "Dry it up before I give you something to cry about." At recess, when I organized the game, someone whispered, "She's bossy." Every correction reminded me that my voice was too loud, my feelings too big, my presence too sharp.

At home the message sounded different, but it carried the same sting. My mom would sigh when I walked into a room talking too fast, too animated, and too eager. "Lower your voice, Rashida. Why are you always so loud?" My sister would roll her eyes when I cried over something small, calling me dramatic. Even in the place that was supposed to be safest, I learned that shrinking myself was the easier path. That lesson burrowed into my body. My shoulders rounded inward, my laughter cut short. I picked outfits that blended into the background, even when my spirit wanted to shine. Sometimes I would fold my favorite clothes at the bottom of the drawer, hiding them from myself as if keeping them out of sight would protect me from rejection. The world never had to tell me twice. I caught on quickly—small was safe.

Slowly, I learned that belonging wasn't about being myself. It was about trimming pieces off. I muted my laugh, softened my voice, hid the brightness that came naturally. I studied the way other girls crossed their legs, how they folded their hands neatly in their laps, how they giggled softly instead of laughing loud. I thought if I could blend in better, maybe I wouldn't feel the sting of being "too much."

I became fluent in the art of disappearing in plain sight. By middle school, I could scan a room and know instantly how much of myself was safe to show. I laughed at jokes that cut me, nodded when I wanted to protest, and stayed silent when everything in me wanted to scream: *See me. The real me.* Years later, the habit of shrinking followed me into uniform.

The roll call room was always the same. Rows of chairs, the scuff of boots on tile, the faint crackle of radios carrying unfinished business. The walls held the residue of too many stories we didn't talk about—calls that went bad; faces we couldn't forget. That day, the air was heavier than usual, thick with the kind of silence that comes after something you can't undo. We were debriefing a call from the night before—a messy one, full of split-second choices that blurred the line between right and wrong, duty and regret.

An officer across the room told his version of what happened. His words were steady, confident, but I knew he was missing critical details. I had been there too. I had seen the way the suspect's hands shook, the hesitation in our approach, the choice that shifted everything. My chest tightened. *Say something, I told myself. Correct it. Clarify.* My hand even twitched, ready to rise. But then I caught the sideways glances around the room, the smirks when someone else spoke up too bluntly, the quick roll of eyes when someone challenged the narrative. I remembered every time I had been told I was "too direct," every warning to "pick your battles."

I stayed quiet. Kept my face neutral, even as my jaw locked so tight it pulsed behind my ears. My silence gave his version power, and with it, I felt my own truth start to fade. The sergeant moved on. The room exhaled. Laughter flickered back to life, chairs scraped against the floor and everyone carried on like nothing had been lost. But something had—something I couldn't name yet, but felt leave the room with me.

Walking out, the weight sat heavy on my chest. The echo of my unsaid words followed me into the hallway, into my patrol car, into the drive home. The city outside blurred past my windshield, but I barely saw it. My hands gripped the wheel tightly. My jaw locked. I drove in silence, radio off, the conversation looping over and over in my mind.

That night, I couldn't sleep. I replayed the scene again and again, whispering the words I wished I had said. My body wouldn't rest, my jaw grinding in the dark, my shoulders stiff against the pillow. I woke before the alarm, still tense, still heavy, like I had fought a battle no one else even knew had happened. That is the cost of shrinking; your body pays for the words your mouth refuses to release.

When I finally walked inside the next afternoon, my daughter was waiting with a backpack too big for her frame, bouncing on her toes. She climbed into the back sea, chattering about her day, her science project, her friend who made her laugh, and what she wanted for dinner. I nodded, smiling, but a piece of me was still in that room, still muted, still erased. No one else noticed, but I did.

That silence wasn't neutral. It cost me. Each time I swallowed my voice, I felt myself shrinking smaller and smaller inside the very uniform that was supposed to give me authority. Authority on the outside meant nothing if I kept erasing myself on the inside. Silence didn't just live in roll call—it followed me home, into my relationships, where shrinking became another kind of survival.

There was one night I remember too clearly when I finally worked up the courage to tell someone I loved that I needed more. More consistency, more honesty, more of him showing up. I had rehearsed the words all day, whispering them to myself in the mirror, trying to keep them steady. When they finally came out, my voice shook anyway.

He sighed, leaning back, his eyes flicking away like my needs were a nuisance. "You always want too much," he said. The words landed heavier than he realized. *Too much.* That old familiar refrain. I felt my body fold in on itself. My chest ached as if my ribs were closing in. My hands twisted in my lap, searching for somewhere safe to put all that nervous energy. My heart wanted to argue, to insist that what I asked for was the bare minimum, not excess. But instead I softened my tone, made a joke, tried to ease the tension. I told myself keeping the peace was safer than risking the loss.

Later, lying awake beside him, I stared at the ceiling and replayed the moment the same way I replayed roll call. The pause before I spoke. The way my truth came out small. The speed with which I tucked it away again after his sigh. Once again, I had chosen silence over self. Once again, I had shrunk. I didn't know another way until years later, when I found myself in a women's support group. I told myself I was just there to listen—armor still in place. My badge wasn't on, but my silence still was.

The room was softly lit, the air thick with something unspoken. A circle of folding chairs waited in the center—too close for comfort, too open to hide. On a table nearby sat tea, tissues, and a neat stack of notebooks for anyone brave enough to put their truth on paper.

I hovered at the edge, pretending to study the room while trying to steady my breath. Every detail felt intentional, like the space itself knew what I'd come here to do—break open just a little. When I finally sat down, I chose a chair close enough to be seen, but far enough to disappear if I needed to. When it came time to introduce myself, I gave the room my name, my profession, a light joke to deflect. People chuckled politely. My smile held, but it was only a shield.

Then a woman across from me began to speak. Her voice shook as she talked about her desire to be seen, about wanting the world to remember her name. She admitted that she had stayed quiet for too long, afraid of what people might think. She looked nothing like me, but her words named pieces of my story.

My throat tightened. My palms pressed hard against my knees. My heart pounded loud enough that I was sure someone could hear it. I wanted to speak, but fear pinned me in place. I stayed quiet. But I stayed. And that choice—to remain in the room even in silence—was the first crack in the armor I had worn for so long. I came back the next week. And the next. Each time I fought the urge to shrink into safety.

Until one night, without planning, my voice broke open. I don't remember everything I said. What I do remember is how it felt in my body. My hands shook, my throat burned, my words tumbled out too fast to catch. I talked about silence. About loss. About being tired of pretending I was fine. I braced myself for rejection—for someone to roll their eyes the way classmates once had, for someone to sigh the way he had.

But no one left. No one told me I was too much. They didn't have perfect answers, but they leaned in. One woman handed me a tissue without a word. Another whispered, "Me too." Their presence told me what my shrinking had always hidden from me: that I was never alone in wanting to be seen. That staying is sometimes the most sacred response.

When the meeting ended, I sat in my car gripping the steering wheel, tears sliding silently down my cheeks. My body still trembled, but it wasn't from fear anymore, it was release. For the first time in years, I said my truth out loud—and the world didn't end. In fact, something had begun. I drove home in silence, but this time it wasn't heavy. It was holy. It was then I learned that performance might keep people around, but presence is what makes them stay.

I am still unlearning the reflex to disappear. Sometimes I still feel the pull to bite back the truth for the sake of peace. But now I catch myself. I breathe. I remind myself that my presence is not a burden. My wholeness is not too much. The right people will never ask me to make myself small in order to be loved.

Because real belonging begins inside me. It is the decision to show up whole, even when my body remembers every moment it was unsafe to do so. Even when silence still feels easier. Belonging begins when I belong to myself first.

But that night, as I got ready for a work event, I reached for a yellow dress. Bright and alive with color. The kind of dress that announced itself before I ever said a word. The fabric shimmered when it caught the light. It hugged my frame in places I once tried to cover and flowed free in places I once tried to hide. I thought of the girl who used to reach for gray sweaters to blend in, who believed muted colors could protect her. Now here I was, slipping into a color that carried no apology.

When I walked into the room, I felt the familiar urge to shrink, to smooth myself back into the edges. But the dress wouldn't let me. It moved when I moved, demanded to be seen. For once, I didn't hide. I smiled, introduced myself, let my laughter fill the space without scanning the room for permission. Belonging didn't come from who noticed me—it came from knowing I no longer needed to disappear.

For a moment, the old voices tried to creep back in. *It's too much. You're too loud. Tone it down.* But then I caught my own reflection. The way the fabric caught the light. The way my shoulders held steady. And I smiled. When I walked into the room, heads turned.

Not in mockery. Not in whispers. Just in acknowledgment. I felt every eye and didn't shrink. I lifted my chin, let my laughter carry, and stayed fully present in my own skin. Someone reached for me in conversation, and I leaned in without apology.

I felt joy. Not just relief at being seen, but joy in allowing myself to shine. That, to me, is freedom. Not just knowing I don't have to shrink, but choosing not to, over and over again. I have been called extra. I have been told I was too much. For a long time, I believed it. But now I see those words differently. Extra means overflowing. Too much means abundant. If that is what I am, then let me be all of it. Loud. Bold. Unapologetic.

I once learned translation as survival. Now I am learning presence as freedom. Because I am no longer shrinking. And that, finally, is freedom. And when Kenzie looks at me now, I want her to see more than the armor I once wore. I want her to see a mother who takes up space, who wears color without apology, who tells the truth even when her voice shakes. Kenzie smiled down at me, her height a quiet reminder of how much she had grown. "You look so pretty, Mommy," she said before leaning in to kiss my forehead. I closed my eyes, holding onto the sweetness of the moment, and whispered back, "So do you."

I want her to inherit fullness, not smallness. I want her to know she is allowed to take up every inch of the space God gave her. Because the cycle breaks with me. That night in my yellow dress, I felt whole—unhidden, unashamed. But freedom without connection still left room to grow. I had learned how to belong to myself; now it was time to learn how to love without the armor that once kept me safe.

CHAPTER 19

Love Without Armor

*The presence that mattered more
than the protection I clung to*

LOVE WITHOUT ARMOR DIDN'T ERASE THE SCARS. It simply said: you are safe to show them. And in letting myself be seen, I began to believe softness was not my enemy—it was my freedom. There was a night I'll never forget. We were lying in bed. Not speaking. Not touching. Just breathing in the quiet between us. The lights were off. The room was still. There was no threat, no raised voice, no tension. But also, no peace. He reached for my hand, and I pulled away. Not sharply, but instinctively, like a reflex from a wound I hadn't named yet. "I'm sorry," I said, not even sure what for. He looked at me softly and replied, "You don't have to be sorry for protecting yourself."

In that moment, something connected—not all at once—but enough to make me realize I didn't know how not to protect myself. I didn't know how to receive love without preparing to lose it. I didn't know how to rest inside someone's tenderness without bracing for the fall. Learning to let someone touch the parts of me that weren't just skin, but story—that was the real intimacy I never saw coming. The kind that doesn't start with hands or heat, but with presence. With stillness. With the quiet courage to sit in the spaces I usually guard.

There's a sacredness in the pauses between words; in the silence that doesn't rush to be filled, in the way someone reaches for you—not to change you, not to rescue you, but simply to stay close. To witness. That kind of intimacy—the kind that sees you without demanding anything in return—used to terrify me, because it asked for the one thing I spent a lifetime protecting: my truth.

Real intimacy means being seen. And being seen means being known. And being known meant letting someone trace their fingers across the scar tissue I had spent years trying to hide. I thought I had done the work. I thought surviving the trauma was enough—that naming my wounds in therapy, finding the language for my pain, and learning how to speak my truth meant I was ready: ready for a love that was soft, steady, and safe. A love that didn't require performance. A love I didn't have to chase.

But readiness is not the same as openness. When love finally came, not with grand gestures but with quiet consistency, I realized how much of me still lived behind glass. The armor had cost me more than I realized. I had spent years lying next to people and still feeling alone, my back turned, my body curled tight, as if distance could shield me. I laughed at the right times, made love when it was expected, played the part of "easy to handle" even when my chest ached with unshed words.

Silence had become my second skin; independence, my only currency. I called it strength, but most nights it felt like isolation. And part of that wasn't just mine. It was inherited. I grew up watching women survive without being held—my grandmother, who buried her grief in chores; my mother, who worked herself raw and never cried where we could see. They were praised for their endurance, for their ability to carry the load without ever laying it down. Black women are often told our strength is our crown, but no one tells us that the crown is heavy—or that sometimes it cuts into our scalp.

I never saw rest celebrated. I never saw tenderness modeled as safety. The women around me had learned to survive by staying guarded—protecting themselves with silence, with steel, with control. So when intimacy came knocking, when someone whispered, you're safe here, I didn't know how to believe it. Safety wasn't a language I grew up speaking; it was one I had to learn, slowly, like translation through trembling hands.

There was a night when all the fear I'd been holding in finally erupted. Tears poured so fast I couldn't catch them. My chest heaved. My words tumbled out between gasps: I can't do this. I'm too much. You're going to leave. Everyone leaves. I tried to pull away, fists pressed into his chest, pushing against the very closeness I craved. His shirt was damp from my tears, my sobs loud in the dark.

He didn't loosen his arms or lecture. He didn't run. He simply stayed. And in that staying, something shifted again. Intimacy revealed itself not in fireworks or perfect moments, but in a steady presence strong enough to hold me when I unraveled. That night taught me that intimacy is not about never breaking. It is about having somewhere safe to land when you do. The old me would have grabbed my keys, driven until the tank ran dry, and swallowed the tears until they burned holes inside me. The healing me stayed. I stayed, even when every part of me wanted to run.

I confused intimacy with sex, believing that offering my body might fill the quiet spaces where no one ever stayed. I remember one night, long before this love, lying beside a man who fell asleep almost instantly after we were done. I lay wide awake, staring at the ceiling, my skin still damp, my heart heavy. He had gotten what he wanted. I had given what I thought might tether him to me. But when the room fell quiet, the emptiness was louder than his snores.

That was the night I first understood: you can share a bed—share your skin—and still live like strangers. I carried that emptiness into other moments too. Once, a man reached to brush the hair from my face, and I flinched before I could stop myself. It wasn't violent, it wasn't threatening, but my body recoiled as if tenderness itself were dangerous. Even hugs felt like negotiations. I'd stiffen, count the seconds, pull away before the warmth could sink in. My body was fluent in defense but foreign in rest.

And it wasn't just mine. I learned it from the world around me. Black women are taught to survive, not to soften. We're told to hold families together, to shoulder grief quietly, to never need too much. In uniforms and boardrooms, in relationships and friendships, strength is demanded first, humanity second. No wonder intimacy felt foreign to me. I hadn't just armored myself; I had inherited the armor. What I had been chasing all those years wasn't sex at all. It was connection. And connection requires more than skin. It requires surrender. It requires trust. With him, I started to test that trust. There were setbacks. Nights when, after sex, I rolled to the edge of the bed, curling into myself as if disappearing could protect me. Mornings where I'd apologize for my tears, as if softness were spills someone else had to mop up.

But there were sacred wins too: the time I let him hold me while I cried and didn't apologize. The time I told him about a childhood memory I'd never said out loud, and he just listened—no advice, no fixing, just presence. The time I didn't flinch when he touched my face, and I didn't overthink why. Healing didn't make intimacy easy. It made it honest. And honesty, I learned, is its own kind of sacred touch.

Not all lessons came through rupture. Some came in the ordinary. We were in the kitchen, washing dishes. Music low, the smell of garlic and onions still hanging in the air. He stood beside me, quietly rinsing a plate, humming along to the radio. At one point, without thinking, I leaned against him. Just leaned, hip to hip, shoulder to shoulder. And he didn't move away.

No words. No questions. Just the steady rhythm of water, the warmth of another body beside mine. I noticed my shoulders drop, my breath lengthen, the tightness in my jaw loosen for the first time that day. My body—traitor to my fears—was learning safety before my mind did. I let out a laugh, light and unexpected, when he sang off-key to the chorus without missing a beat. It wasn't the sound of hollow politeness; it was real, rising from somewhere unguarded. And in that stillness—in that laughter—I realized: intimacy doesn't always announce itself. Sometimes it's just the permission to rest for five minutes in someone's presence without fear.

That night, I laughed easier. And my laughter didn't sound hollow anymore. There was another night when intimacy came knocking, but it wasn't from a partner. It was from my daughter. Kenzie must have been eight or nine at the time. She had a nightmare and padded down the hall to my room, her hair wild from tossing, her blanket dragging behind her like a cape. She didn't say anything at first, just stood in the doorway, eyes wide, waiting to see if she was welcome.

"Come on," I said, lifting the covers. My voice sounded softer than I felt. Inside, my body braced. Even with my own child, I wasn't always comfortable with closeness. She climbed into bed and curled against me, her breath warm on my arm. I lay still, staring at the ceiling, every muscle taut. The old armor whispered: Don't get used to this. Don't lean too hard. You'll be left holding the weight alone.

But then she reached for my hand the same way he had, small fingers sliding into mine, and whispered, "Don't let go." Something inside me fractured then rearranged. My first instinct was to keep my grip loose, just in case she shifted away. But she held on tighter, anchoring herself to me like I was the only safe place in the world.

That's when I realized my daughter wasn't asking for a protector or a provider in that moment. She was asking for presence. She was asking me to stay. I thought about my own childhood, how I never crawled into my mother's bed after nightmares, how tears were tucked away before they could be seen. No one had ever held me, through the dark. And here was my daughter, reaching for something I never knew how to ask for, something I was still learning how to give.

Her breathing slowed as she drifted back to sleep, her small chest rising and falling against mine. I didn't move, even when my arm went numb, even when the weight of her body pressed heavy into me. I stayed. I let her stay. The room was quiet except for her breath and the faint hum of the world outside. And for once, I didn't retreat into the safety of distance. I let softness have me.

I felt my heartbeat slow to match hers, my lungs unclench, my body surrender to the quiet rhythm of belonging. That night taught me that intimacy is not just about romance, or even adulthood—it's about showing up in the quiet, ordinary hours when someone you love needs your softness more than your strength. My daughter didn't want explanations. She didn't want me to be strong. She wanted to be held. And in choosing to hold her, I was also learning how to hold myself.

But here's the mirror I had to face: it wasn't just that I didn't trust closeness. I didn't trust me to be loved. I didn't trust that I was worth staying for. I didn't trust that my tears wouldn't drown the people closest to me. I didn't trust that my truth—unpolished, unperformed, unarmored—was enough.

Every flinch, every apology, every instinct to retreat was less about him and more about me. More about the girl who learned that needing was dangerous. More about the woman who confused independence with invisibility. The hardest truth was this: I wasn't learning to trust him. I was learning to trust myself with love. Sometimes healing looks like fireworks. Mine looked like falling asleep with my guard down, my face wet with tears, my hand unclenched against his chest. No performance. Just presence.

And in that stillness, I understood: love without armor doesn't erase the scars. It simply says, you are safe to show them. I think about what it means for my daughter to see me soften. For her to see a love that doesn't demand silence, that doesn't punish tears. For her to know from the start that being seen isn't dangerous.

Loving without armor isn't just for me. It's for her. It's for the women before me who called survival love because it was all they were given. And it's for the girl I used to be—the one who thought being unhidden was too dangerous to survive. This is the gift: not a perfect love, but a present one. A love that lets you rest. A love that lets you breathe. A love that lets you be.

For so long, I thought intimacy began with someone else. But the hardest reckoning came when I realized the person I had been running from was myself. Before I could relearn closeness, I had to return to my own heart, to the parts that never learned how to rest in love, the parts that mistook proving for belonging. It wasn't another's touch that healed me. It was the slow, tender work of believing I was worthy of love even when no one else was in the room. Of offering myself the same presence I once begged others to stay for.

That, I have learned, is what it means to love without armor: to meet yourself without performance, to stay when the silence feels heavy. To let softness do the work that strength never could. Love taught me how to stay. Softness would teach me why.

CHAPTER 20

What Softness Revealed

The strength I found in finally laying my guard down

SOFTNESS DID NOT MAKE ME WEAK. It made me whole. It reminded me that strength lives in both the breaking and the rising, in the ache and the hope. And in that truth, I found a new way to carry myself—lighter, freer, still standing. The call was quiet on paper. No sirens cutting the night. No chase. Just a living room that smelled like old carpet and something fried hours ago, a hallway light left on, a television murmuring to no one. The arrest was by the book; cuffs, forms, a small nod between officers that meant keep it steady. I knew the motions. My face did what it was trained to do: calm and composed.

What I was not ready for was the sound that came out of his daughter. She could not have been more than seven. She wrapped both arms around his leg, fingers clutching denim like she could anchor him with the force of her grip. Her shoulders shook. She tried to climb higher, as if reaching his waist could stop time. When she looked up at me, her eyes were wide and wet, the kind of pleading that finds the hollow places you have worked hard to ignore.

Do you see me, her face asked. Do you see what this is doing to me. My chest tightened until it felt too small for my lungs. My throat burned as if it was holding back both words and sobs. My hands, so steady with cuffs and forms, wanted to tremble. I locked my jaw, not to stay professional, but to keep from breaking in front of her. I wanted to pick her up. I wanted to promise something I could not promise. The badge asked me for composure. My body asked me to be human. I chose the job. I spoke softly, words that fell flat in a room heavy with rupture. The door closed behind us. The paperwork moved forward. The house grew still again. I drove away with my jaw tight and my hands gripping the wheel too firmly.

I made it two blocks before the tears came. They fell hard and quick, like they had been waiting at a gate. Shame tried to climb into the seat beside me. You do not get to fall apart. Be strong. Handle it. The words sounded familiar, a chorus I had lived by. Another voice, smaller but steady, rose to meet them. You are human. This hurts because you can feel. That is not failure. That is proof of life.

I believed strength meant swallowing the ache before it reached my eyes. It meant carrying my own weight—and yours too—without ever letting my hands shake. That kind of strength kept me moving, but it also kept me alone. I wore it like a uniform beneath the uniform—starched, heavy, and suffocating. It rubbed raw in places no one could see.

I did not learn that version of strength in a training block. I learned it at home. There is a quieter story that lives under the loud ones, the kind you do not remember until your body does. I was maybe seven or eight, roller skating too fast on cracked pavement. One wheel caught the edge of the sidewalk, and I went down hard. My knee tore open, pebbles pressed into the scrape like small moons. I walked inside, trying not to cry. The kitchen smelled like baked chicken and mashed potatoes. My mother looked up, tired from a long day—her eyes a mixture of love and a thousand things to do.

You are fine, she said. Clean it up. Be careful next time. She was not cruel. She was efficient, focused, a woman doing her best to hold the house together. Tenderness did not have much room to live in our schedule. I learned to wash my own knee. I learned to walk away before anyone could see me wince. I learned to take pride in not needing help.

And yet, I remember one night when I was sick with the flu. Fever hot, sheets damp, body too heavy to move. My mother pressed a cool washcloth to my forehead. She didn't say much, just left her hand there longer than usual. It startled me more than it comforted me. I wanted it to last, and I didn't trust that it would. That fleeting moment stayed lodged in me, proof that softness existed, but also proof of how quickly it could vanish.

Years later, the lesson looked polished. Promotions. Commendations. The name on the uniform sitting just right. I could power through anything, or at least that was the story. Grief made a liar out of me. It sat quiet in my body, heavy as wet wool, and when I tried to outwork it, it only got louder. That little girl at the call showed me the part I kept refusing to see. Some pain is not meant to be managed. It is meant to be met.

There is a couch I know well. Neutral fabric, the kind with a texture that almost hides the pulls. The hum of a white noise machine behind the door. My therapist sits in her chair, and waits me out. I spend the first ten minutes talking like I am filing a report. Timeline. Facts. Minimal adjectives. She listens. Then she asks the question she always asks when my words try to outrun my feelings.

Where is it in your body right now. I hate that question, and I need it. I close my eyes and search. Tight jaw. Shoulders that live near my ears. A chest that forgets how to rise. She tells me to breathe into the place that is clenched. I do not want to. I do it anyway. The first breath shudders. The second finds a little space. The third reaches deeper than I expect. My throat burns. My eyes sting. I let the tears come. It is not cinematic. There is no music. Just the quiet of a room where no one needs me to be anything but honest.

We talk about the call. We talk about the girl. We talk about how the child in me recognizes the child in her. We talk about the knee that learned to stop asking to be tended. She says a thing I write down later because I do not want to forget it. The parts of you that kept you alive deserve a thank-you. They do not have to drive anymore.

That is what softness began to reveal. Not an erasing of strength; a reassigning. I could keep the steadiness that serves me, and let go of the hardness that isolates me. I could honor the muscle that carried me through and still choose to rest. I could stop leading with my armor and start leading with my truth.

But learning to find softness in myself was only part of the work. The harder part came when that softness appeared in someone else's hands, warm and steady, and I didn't know if I could trust it. There was a night when softness filled the room—gentle, patient, unassuming—and I almost sent it away. Not because I didn't want it, but because I didn't yet believe I deserved it.

We were not fighting. There was no tension in the air, no words left unsaid. Just a long day, the kind that leaves your shoulders heavy, your mind buzzing even as the house quiets. I was lying on the couch, one arm draped across my stomach, pretending to scroll my phone. He sat beside me, close but not touching, and I could feel him watching me out of the corner of his eye. "You're quiet," he said. Not accusing; not prying. Just noticing. "I'm fine," I answered, the old script spilling out of my mouth before I even thought about it. The two words landed flat between us.

He did not argue. He did not ask again. Instead, he leaned in, slow and steady, and placed his hand on my cheek. His thumb brushed just under my eye, tracing a line as if he could wipe away something he could not name. Everything in me tensed. My body registered danger before my mind could reason. I wanted to pull away, to laugh it off, to distract him with a story or a joke. Softness like that had always felt suspicious. A touch that gentle had never been safe in my story.

But I didn't move. Not right away. I stayed still, heart pounding, chest tight, every nerve on alert. He must have felt the stiffness in me, because he didn't press closer. He just kept his hand there, warm and steady, like he was waiting for me to decide if I could bear it. The silence stretched long. My throat ached with all the words I didn't know how to say: I don't know how to be held like this. I don't know if I deserve it. I don't know if I can stay.

Finally, the truth slipped out in a whisper so soft I almost didn't hear myself. "This is hard for me." His hand didn't move. His voice was low and even. "I know." I let out a shaky breath, the kind you don't realize you've been holding for years. My jaw unclenched. My shoulders dropped. For the first time in a long time, I didn't turn away. I let his palm stay against my face. I let myself be seen, right there in my unease.

That night taught me something I had never understood before: softness could feel like confrontation. Not with him, but with myself. Every gentle touch, every patient silence, every invitation to rest forced me to face the parts of me that didn't believe I was worthy of it. Softness wasn't threatening because of what it was. It was threatening because of what it revealed. It revealed how long I had gone without it. It revealed how much I still feared losing it. It revealed how much of me still braced for abandonment, even in the middle of being cared for.

There were other nights like that. Nights when I cried into his shirt and then immediately tried to apologize, to mop myself up before I made too much of a mess. Nights when he would kiss my forehead and I'd stiffen, my body translating tenderness as danger. Nights when he would reach for my hand in public, and I would look around, embarrassed by the simple act of being loved out loud.

But there were also small victories. The first time I rested my head on his chest and actually let myself stay there. The first time I fell asleep in his arms without waking in the middle of the night to roll away. The first time I laughed, really laughed, at something ridiculous, he said, without covering it up, without worrying if I sounded too loud, too much. Each of those moments chipped away at the old armor. Not all at once. Not clean or easy. But enough to show me that softness didn't have to mean danger. It could mean safety. It could mean home.

Softness also arrived wearing a child's pajamas. Kenzie woke from a bad dream and stood in my doorway with her blanket bunched in her fists. I lifted the covers and she climbed in. Her hair smelled like coconut and sleep. She tucked herself against me, small and sure. I have spent years bracing without realizing it, muscles on standby even at rest. That night I noticed my body do something different. My breathing found hers. My jaw unclenched. My hand stayed open in hers. She whispered do not let go. I did not.

I wish I could say I became a new person all at once. I did not. Change arrived like Seattle rain, light then steady, then all at once when you are standing in it. The work looked ordinary from the outside. Saying no without apology. Leaving a room when my peace cost too much to stay. Taking the long way home on a day my chest felt crowded. Turning my phone face down and choosing silence. Letting laughter be a full sound and not a covering.

Power changed shape too. It stopped being a performance and started being a practice. Sometimes power sounded like I do not need to win this, I need to be well. Sometimes it looked like ending a conversation that was only about who could talk over whom. Sometimes it meant telling the truth without padding it for comfort, then letting the silence do what it does.

The job did not get softer. People still called on their worst days. Paperwork still stacked in ways that made time feel thin. The city still asked for more than any one person could give. But inside the same days, something in me was different. I could stand in a hard room and not abandon myself. I could feel the ache and not make it the enemy. I could be strong without disappearing.

If you were told that strength means being hard, I understand why. Hardness looks like it works. It gets you through shifts and seasons. It earns applause. It also empties you. Softness is not the opposite of strength. Softness is the depth of it. Softness is the breath that keeps you from burning out while you hold what matters. Softness is the permission to put down what was never yours to lift.

Grief taught me that. It did not ask for a polished answer. It asked for presence. It asked for patience when nothing changed as fast as I wanted it to. It asked me to tell the truth about what hurt and to let that truth move through me instead of calcifying inside me. It asked me to believe that feeling deeply would not undo me. It did not. It remade me.

There are days now when I still feel the old armor reach for me. My jaw tightens. My shoulders lift. My voice gets clipped. I know what that is. I pause. I name it. I choose again. Sometimes I need help to do that. Sometimes I text a friend and say I am spiraling, can you remind me of what is true. Sometimes I sit in my car for five quiet minutes before walking into a room that expects me to be unshakeable. Sometimes I let Kenzie wrap her arms around me, and I do not make a joke or change the subject. I let the hug last until both of us exhale.

Strength used to be what I could carry. Now it's how gently I can set things down. Strength used to be the story I told to prove I was still standing. Now it's the way I honor the parts of me that needed to rest. Strength once needed an audience. Now it lives in the quiet—something I practice when no one is watching.

I think about that little girl often. The house. The denim. The sound of her crying. I could not fix what broke in front of her. I still cannot fix most of what breaks. But I can refuse to turn away. I can bring a kind of presence that does not solve and still matters. I can be the adult who sees. I can be a mother who lets softness live in our house on regular days, not just on birthdays and holidays, so my daughter never has to wonder if tenderness is allowed.

Softness revealed that my power was never in how tightly I held myself together. It was in how willing I was to be whole, which is different from being unbroken. Whole means I can carry grief and still choose joy. Whole means I can be tired and still be kind. Whole means I can be unsure and still move. Whole means I can be soft and still be strong. I did not stop being the woman who shows up. I stopped making her show up alone. And that, more than anything I could lift or outrun, is what power looks like now. That is what grief and healing revealed: that real power was never in the hardness I carried, but in the softness I finally allowed. Softness revealed new strength, but letting go was its own act of power.

Softness revealed that my power was never in how tightly I held myself together. It was in how willing I was to be whole—which is different from being unbroken. Whole means I can carry grief and still choose joy. Whole means I can be tired and still be kind.

Whole means I can be unsure and still move. Whole means I can be soft and still be strong.

I did not stop being the woman who shows up. I stopped making her show up alone. And that, more than anything I could lift or outrun, is what power looks like now. That is what grief and healing revealed: that real power was never in the hardness I carried, but in the softness I finally allowed. Softness revealed new strength—but letting go was its own act of power.

And somewhere in that letting go, I found my way back to myself. Not the version shaped by survival, but the one who could finally rest inside her own skin. The one who no longer needed to earn peace, only to return to it. This was the beginning of my homecoming.

PART V

The Homecoming

The silence remade, the fire still burning,
the light finally let in

The journey was never about erasing scars but
learning to live within them without hiding.

Coming home meant laying down the armor,
forgiving what fractured me, and finally
remembering that peace had always
been possible.

It was softer than I imagined,
and stronger than I'd ever been.

CHAPTER 21

Letting the Light In

The windows I once boarded shut
against tenderness and love

I DON'T REMEMBER WHAT SONG was playing that afternoon, only the sound of Kenzie's laugh, high and unrestrained, bouncing off the walls of our living room. She twirled in circles, arms stretched wide, her little body moving with a freedom I had never known at her age. "Dance with me, Mommy!" she shouted, tugging at my hand. For a second, I hesitated. My instinct was to stay seated, to watch instead of join. Survival had trained my body to stay tight, controlled, always ready. Joy was a language I hadn't spoken in years. But there was something about the way her braids swung, beads clattering like laughter, her eyes locked on mine, daring me to soften. I stood up. And I let go.

At first, my movements were stiff, calculated, knees bending reluctantly, feet searching for rhythm. But Kenzie's laughter drowned out my hesitation. Her palm was small but insistent, pulling me deeper into her orbit. We spun across the hardwood floor, socks sliding, arms flailing, our laughter colliding until I couldn't tell which belonged to her and which belonged to me. It wasn't graceful. It wasn't practiced. But it was real, messy, full-bodied, alive. I didn't care how it looked or if the neighbors could hear.

Something in my chest split wide, and a sound escaped me I hadn't heard in years: an unguarded laugh, the kind that shook me from the inside out.

That moment broke something in me—but in the best way. Because the truth is, joy had always felt foreign, like a language I wasn't fluent in. I had spent so many years translating survival that joy felt too tender, too light to trust. It startled me with its ease, the way it asked nothing of me but presence. I didn't know how to hold something that didn't hurt.

Growing up, laughter came in short bursts, quickly swallowed by silence or survival. I remember one evening when my sister and I tried to make each other laugh at the dinner table. We pressed our hands over our mouths to keep the giggles from spilling out too loud, our shoulders shaking, eyes wet with the effort of holding it in. The smell of fried chicken and collard greens hung in the air, plates clattering as forks scraped against them. Just as the laughter was about to boil over, my mom's voice cut through the air, weary but firm: "Quiet down." Not cruel, just tired. The laughter stopped instantly. Smiles folded away like napkins, tucked neatly back into silence.

That's what joy felt like in our house, rationed, like sugar during hard times. A little was allowed, but too much made people nervous, as if it would draw the wrong kind of attention or tempt fate to remind us of our place. I never saw anyone dancing barefoot in the kitchen, not without a reason to celebrate. And even then, the celebration was short-lived, shadowed by what might come next.

As I grew older, I treated joy like a privilege, not a practice. Something you could touch only after the work was done, after the bills were paid, after the grief had quieted. A reward, not a right. When joy showed up in my adult life, it felt suspicious. My body didn't trust it. My chest tightened in the middle of laughter, my shoulders braced, as if joy itself were dangerous. Because trauma rewires you that way. It convinces you that joy is bait, a trick, a setup for the fall. You start to believe that laughter is temporary and vigilance permanent. So even when I laughed, I kept a part of me on edge, scanning for the moment it would end.

And when someone asked me how I was, the answer was always ready: *I'm fine.* It rolled off my tongue without thought, stitched into my jaw, my shoulders, my smile. *I'm fine* meant, Don't look too close. *I'm fine* meant, Don't ask me to lay anything down. I said it at roll call, when exhaustion sat heavy in my bones. I said it in relationships, when I was unraveling inside. I even said it in therapy, turning my pain into performance. *I'm fine* was my mother's voice in my throat, my grandmother's silence pressed into my skin, my own fear that if I cracked, the whole world would shatter with me.

Still, there were times it felt almost shameful. There were nights I'd come home from a shift, still carrying the image of someone's son in handcuffs, someone's daughter crying on the curb, someone's mother collapsing at the sight of a sheet pulled over a body. The weight of it all clung to me like smoke. I would strip off my vest, unbuckle my duty belt, and stand for a moment in the dark hallway, unable to reconcile the two worlds I lived in. Then I'd push the door open and step inside, where cartoons flickered on the television, the smell of popcorn filled the air, and Kenzie came running, arms outstretched, laughter spilling out of her like sunlight.

Part of me wanted to scoop her up, to match her light, but another part of me stiffened, like I didn't deserve it. How could I let myself laugh when somebody else's mother was grieving? How could I spin in circles in my kitchen when just hours before I stood in the wreckage of someone else's worst day?

That's the part of joy people don't talk about: the guilt. The fear that if you let joy in, it means you've forgotten the weight you carry. That it means you've betrayed your pain, or worse, the pain of others. For a long time, I thought joy made me unfaithful to grief. But the truth is, joy was never a betrayal. It was proof I was still alive. And sometimes joy felt so sharp it cut me open.

Once, Kenzie and I laughed so hard in the kitchen that I doubled over, clutching my stomach, and suddenly the laughter turned into tears. She thought I was still laughing, but what she didn't know was that joy had broke open a door grief had been holding shut. Tears poured out, hot and unstoppable, even as the sound of her giggles kept floating through the room. And maybe that's what joy does. It doesn't erase the ache. It lets it breathe. It reminds you that sorrow and laughter can live in the same body, in the same breath.

And other times, joy refused to arrive at all. There were mornings when the weight of everything I carried pressed me so deep into the couch that I didn't think I could rise. I scrolled on my phone, numbing myself, while Kenzie tugged at my sleeve, "Come play, Mommy. Come dance." I almost told her no, told her I was too tired, too busy, too everything. But her persistence split open my armor, and eventually, I stood. The first few steps were heavy, but as her laughter filled the room, my body remembered what my mind had forgotten: joy isn't something we wait for, it's something we step into. And sometimes, it takes a child's hand to remind you that moving is its own kind of miracle.

And for me, as a Black woman, as a mother, as an officer, choosing joy became an act of defiance. The world expected me to carry grief. To shoulder pain without complaint. To be strong, stoic, unshaken. But laughing loudly, dancing freely, letting my daughter see softness in me—that was rebellion. That was resistance. That was freedom in its purest form.

I think about the women who came before me. My grandmother burying her grief in chores, humming low under her breath as if music might keep the silence from swallowing her whole. My mother working herself raw and never crying where we could see. Their strength was real, but it came at a cost. They were praised for their endurance, but no one ever asked what it cost them to never lay it down. No one celebrated their rest. No one gave them permission to laugh until their bellies hurt.

And yet, even in those heavy years, joy found ways to slip through the cracks. At family cookouts, when the grill smoked and somebody turned the music up, the older women would tap their feet, their shoulders swaying before they realized they were moving. The bass from the speakers thumped against our chests, cousins raced through the grass, and for a brief moment the air felt lighter, as if all of us had agreed to set down what we carried just long enough to breathe. At church, joy rose from the choir stands, tambourines shaking, hands clapping, voices so loud they rattled the windows. The sound was defiant, a reminder that even when the world outside tried to silence us, our joy had its own language.

Joy, I've learned, is never free. It costs you the safety of silence. It costs you the shield of control. It asks you to risk being seen in your fullness, even when the world tells you to shrink. For Black women especially, joy has always been a revolution. It's why we sing loud in sanctuaries, why we dance at cookouts, why we laugh with our whole bodies even when life has tried to break us. Our joy has always been more than a feeling. It has been survival, resistance, and prophecy all at once.

And now, I see myself as part of that lineage. Only this time, I don't want joy to be rationed. I want it to be inherited. I once believed my daughter would never really know me, the me underneath the armor, underneath the badge, underneath all the practiced *I'm fines*. I thought she would inherit only the version of me that kept watch, that stayed on guard, that knew how to endure but not how to exhale. But joy shifted that story.

When Kenzie saw me laugh, really laugh, the kind that bent me over and left tears streaming down my cheeks, she saw a softness I had once thought was lost. She saw a mother who could be silly, who could let go, who could be fully alive in her presence. And in those moments, I realized joy wasn't just for me. It was a legacy. It was what I wanted her to inherit instead of silence.

There are still days when my chest feels heavy, when silence tries to reclaim me. But then there are nights when Kenzie and I dance barefoot in the kitchen, our shadows stretching across the walls, our laughter rising above the low hum of the refrigerator. In those moments, I remember that healing doesn't always look like peace— sometimes it looks like movement, breath, sound. And even when the ache lingers, joy still finds its way home to me.

And sometimes, in the daylight, we wash the car together in the driveway. Kenzie grips the hose with both hands, spraying more water onto herself than the car, laughing as the mist soaks her shirt. I laugh with her, because I finally understand: this is how joy grows. Not in the absence of struggle, but in the choosing. In the tending. In the small, ordinary acts of care. In the willingness to shine light on what we want to flourish and to keep returning, even when it feels fragile. Because survival taught me how to endure. But joy is teaching me how to live.

And joy is not fragile—it is a form of protest. It is a refusal to let the weight of the world decide the fullness of my days. It is what keeps me human when everything else demands I stay hard. When I let the light in, even for just a song's length, even for a plant's small drink, I remember that healing isn't only about what I put down. It's also about what I choose to carry forward. And I choose this: laughter in kitchens, barefoot dancing, joy as resistance, light as legacy.

One evening, long after the music stopped, Kenzie and I kept spinning in slow circles, our socks sliding across the floor, our shadows stretching tall against the walls. Her curls brushed my cheek as she laughed, and the sound spilled through the open window into the night air.

In that moment, I understood—this was survival transformed. Not just breath or endurance—but life, loud, uncontained, and ours. For so long, silence was my first inheritance. Armor was my shield. I'm fine was the script I thought I had to pass down. But my daughter will not inherit silence, and she will not inherit armor. This is the legacy I choose for her: light spilling through the window, laughter strong enough to drown the weight, softness as survival, joy as resistance. And maybe that's the legacy for all of us—to let joy take root where grief once lived, to let our laughter be the loudest proof that we survived.

Joy is proof that the silence has finally given way, that the armor can finally rest, that survival is not the ending, but the doorway back to life. Because joy asks more of me than endurance ever did—it asks me to stay. To breathe. To believe that softness can hold what strength once carried. And to stay, I had to learn something harder than surviving—I had to learn how to let go.

CHAPTER 22

The Grace to Let Go

*The forgiveness I needed to extend
to others and myself*

MY HANDS CURLED INTO FISTS I didn't know how to loosen. My jaw stayed clenched, my breath shallow, my shoulders braced—even in the quiet of my own home. I told myself I was fine. I told myself I didn't need softness, didn't need tenderness, didn't need release. But the truth was, I didn't know how to let go. Letting go doesn't mean forgetting. It doesn't mean pretending the pain never happened or silencing the parts of you that survived it. Letting go means loosening the grip that survival once had on you, even when that grip kept you alive. It is the quiet choice not to live from that place forever.

For me, the doorway to letting go opened through parenting. Not just the logistics of lunches packed, practices attended, and grades monitored, but parenting with intention—with softness, with presence, with a love untied from performance or perfection. That's where I first began to understand what it meant to love without condition—and to be loved not because I was easy to hold, but because I was worth holding. Mess and all.

At first, I thought forgiveness was a finish line. Something you arrived at after enough time passed, after the sting wore off and the ache dulled. I thought forgiveness was something clean, linear, and complete. But I've come to learn that real forgiveness is layered. It's not a single moment; it's a practice. A reckoning. A soft returning to yourself, over and over again, especially when old wounds start whispering louder than they used to.

There are people I swore I'd never forgive—people who left when I needed them most, who disappointed me, who disappeared when I was desperate to be seen. Some didn't mean to cause harm, they just didn't have the tools to stay. Others made choices that carved holes I still trip over. For a long time, I carried them all like evidence—proof that love was unreliable, that presence was temporary, that I was safer expecting absence than hoping for care. Forgiveness felt like surrender, and I had survived too much to risk being that open again. I thought holding on would keep me safe, that anger was armor and distance was control. But all it did was keep the wound fresh, preserved beneath the surface of a life that looked whole.

One of those people was my father. He wasn't there—not in the way I needed. His absence was loud, even when he was technically present. I don't remember him helping with homework or cheering in the stands. I remember sitting on cold bleachers, scanning the crowd for his face, pretending I didn't care when the seat beside my mom stayed empty. I remember birthdays where I blew out candles wondering if he would call, the silence afterward louder than his voice could have ever been. I remember writing "Dad" on school forms and feeling like it was just a word—not a person I could depend on.

Still, I wanted him. I wanted what other kids seemed to have without question—the reassurance of a steady voice, a hand on my shoulder, someone who showed up because I mattered. But what I learned instead was how to hide the wanting. I became good at pretending I didn't need what I needed. I learned to turn disappointment into discipline, and longing into independence.

And then there was the night I buried my face in my pillow so my sister wouldn't hear me cry. I was old enough to know better, but young enough to still ache for him. The house was quiet except for the low hum of the refrigerator down the hall. I pressed my fists against my chest and promised myself I would stop wanting what was never coming. That promise hardened into silence. For years, I told myself it didn't matter—that I didn't care, that I was fine. But beneath that story lived another, a quieter truth I buried under pride and self-protection.

When we began speaking again, it was never dramatic. No sweeping apology. No sudden clarity. Just small beginnings, a phone call on a Sunday, an awkward "How are you?" that felt stiff but sincere, a memory shared that surprised me with how much I still longed to hear it. Slowly, carefully, a thread began to stitch between us. Forgiveness didn't erase the empty bleachers or the birthdays missed. But it made space for something new to grow in the cracks.

Still, I resisted the idea of forgiveness at first. In therapy, when my counselor gently suggested I might need to release some of the anger I carried, I felt my whole body tense. The room went quiet. I could hear the clock ticking on the wall, my own breath shallow, my fingers knotting into fists in my lap. I wanted to say, How dare you? Do you know what silence cost me? Do you know what absence feels like? Forgiveness sounded like letting people off the hook. It sounded like weakness.

I remember leaving one session, slamming my car door shut, gripping the steering wheel so tight my knuckles burned. My chest was hot, my throat closed, my eyes blurred with tears I refused to let fall. "I'm not ready," I muttered. "I may never be ready." I sat in that car until the sun dipped low, anger pressed into every muscle, wondering if I was broken for not wanting to release it. What I didn't understand yet was that forgiveness wasn't about excusing anyone. It was about unburdening myself.

What I didn't expect was how much harder it would be to forgive myself. Forgiving others is difficult enough—it asks you to release what you can't rewrite. But self-forgiveness? That's a different kind of labor. It's the slow, steady work of facing the ways you abandoned yourself while trying to survive.

It is grieving what was done to you while also facing what you did to survive. It is looking yourself in the mirror and confronting the walls you built, the people you pushed away, the parts of you that went silent to stay safe. There were so many moments I shut down when I should have spoken up. Times I said I was fine when I wasn't. I performed strength so well that people stopped asking if I was okay. And the truth is, I don't blame them. I didn't leave room for softness. I didn't know how.

One morning, I stood in front of my bathroom mirror, toothbrush in hand, staring into my own eyes. My reflection looked both familiar and foreign, tired eyes, a clenched jaw, shoulders that sagged even when I tried to square them. I set the toothbrush down and whispered, almost to test if my voice would hold: "I forgive you." The words trembled in my throat, as though my body doubted they could be true. But I said them again. Louder. This time my chest softened. The mirror did not talk back, but my reflection felt less like a stranger and more like someone I was willing to care for.

Self-forgiveness is like that. It doesn't happen all at once. It happens in whispers and repetitions until your body begins to believe you. And the cost of holding it all was steep. It showed up in the headaches that pulsed behind my eyes. In the nights I lay awake, chest tight, replaying arguments I never voiced out loud. In the sharpness of my tone with people I loved, not because of them, but because I had no space left to carry anything else. Holding on became its own kind of prison, silent, suffocating, relentless.

There was one night I'll never forget. Kenzie was twelve, and we had just argued about something small that felt impossibly big in the moment—chores, grades, respect. She stormed to her room, slammed the door, and I sat in my car in the driveway long after the house had gone quiet. My hands gripped the steering wheel until my knuckles ached, my jaw locked, my breath shallow. And then the fear surfaced—the question I didn't want to face: Who am I without this pain? The weight had been my companion for so long. Anger was the armor that kept me standing. Vigilance was my language. Part of me worried that if I let it go, I would disappear with it. Because at least the pain was familiar. At least it gave me something to hold.

The tears came before I could stop them. Hot, relentless, shaking me until my shoulders dropped and my body finally unclenched. And in that moment, I whispered to myself words I had never spoken before: "You don't have to hold it all anymore. You can let this go." That night didn't fix everything. It showed me that letting go wasn't just about the past. It was about choosing, moment by moment, not to pass the same weight forward. It took me years to face the hardest truth: sometimes the person you need to forgive most is yourself.

I had to forgive the girl who learned silence too early. The woman who confused independence with invisibility. The mother who sometimes snapped out of exhaustion, then wept in shame. Forgiveness meant placing a hand on my own heart and whispering, You did the best you could with what you had. You weren't weak. You were surviving.

182

Sometimes, forgiveness needed a ritual. One afternoon, I sat at my kitchen table and wrote a letter—to my younger self, to my father, to anyone I still carried in my chest. I poured out the words I never got to say: the anger, the ache, the longing. When I was done, I folded the paper, walked outside, and lit it. I stood barefoot in the driveway as the smoke curled into the evening sky and whispered, I release you. I release me. It wasn't magic, but my body knew. My jaw loosened. My chest softened. And after years of tightening into fists, my hands finally opened.

Maybe you know this too—that moment when the thing that once protected you becomes the very thing keeping you from breathing. When survival, once your shield, becomes your prison. When the walls you built to keep others out end up keeping you in. Letting go is terrifying because it asks you to step into the unknown. But it is also holy.

Motherhood became my teacher. I learned to love without needing Kenzie to earn it. To rub her back at night simply because she asked. To sit with her sadness without trying to fix it. To show up even when I was exhausted, even when I was met with eye rolls and slammed doors and sharp teenage words that stung. To say, I'm still here, after every disagreement.

I remember one evening in particular. We had argued about homework, and my voice rose sharper than I intended. Her eyes filled with tears, and she turned away. Everything in me wanted to retreat into silence, to let the moment pass without naming it. But instead I walked to her room, sat on the edge of her bed, and whispered, "I'm sorry. I was wrong." At first she stayed quiet, but then she leaned into me, her small frame softening against mine. In that moment, I realized that breaking the cycle wasn't about perfection. It was about presence. Every apology, every second chance, every moment of staying when I wanted to hide was its own act of letting go.

Every time I chose love over perfection, I let go of the rules that raised me. Every time I apologized when I got it wrong, or met her silence with presence, I loosened my grip on old beliefs. I showed both of us that love doesn't have to be earned to be real. Then came joy. I used to think joy had to be earned. That I couldn't feel light until I had sorted out all the darkness. That to laugh was to betray the pain I carried. But joy is not betrayal. Joy is resistance—especially for Black women, joy is sacred. Joy is survival.

I learned this first in church, even if I didn't understand it then. The choir would rise, tambourines shaking, voices lifting so high they rattled the stained-glass windows. My grandmother would sway in her seat, her foot tapping before she even realized it. Outside of church she carried silence, but inside those walls, something broke open. I didn't know it yet, but that was joy as survival.

One night years later, after a long shift, I stood in the kitchen unpacking groceries. The smell of bread and fruit filled the room, the hum of the refrigerator steady behind me. A song came on. I don't remember which one. But I let it play. And before I knew it, my body was moving. Small at first. Then bigger. My boots tapped the tile. My arms swayed. My hips followed the rhythm until the room itself felt alive.

And then, without warning, laughter bubbled up—and just as quickly, tears followed. Because in that moment, I wasn't carrying anyone's grief. I wasn't performing strength. I wasn't waiting for the next blow. I was just me—tired, alive, free. I leaned against the counter, chest heaving, sweat dampening the collar of my shirt. My body felt both lighter and heavier, like it had finally remembered what it was to release. That moment stayed with me not because it erased the pain, but because it reminded me that joy was still possible in the middle of it. Letting go gave me space. Coming home to myself gave me freedom.

Letting go isn't the same as forgetting. It's creating room for something else to live inside you besides pain. It's loosening the weight of what could have been, so your hands are free to hold the beauty of what still is. It's honoring the version of me who survived while gently reminding her she doesn't have to hold everything anymore. And at last, that was enough.

For me, strength looks like softness. Stillness. A breath I don't have to hold. A boundary I don't have to explain. A joy I don't have to apologize for. This isn't the version of strength I was raised with. But it's the one I've chosen. The one I fought for. The one I'm still learning to trust. Letting go didn't make me weak. It made me free.

And it didn't just free me. It freed my daughter from inheriting silence. It freed my community from carrying weight that was never theirs. It freed generations of women in my family who had been praised for their endurance but never allowed to rest. My mother smoked her grief into the night. My grandmother carried her fury in her shoulders, tight and unyielding. My great-grandmother slammed doors and swallowed secrets. They didn't have the luxury of letting go. But I do. And when I soften, I honor them too.

One evening, I sat on the porch as the sun sank low, the air heavy with summer heat. Inside, Kenzie was humming, her voice drifting through the window like a soft hymn. My fists unclenched against my thighs. My chest filled with a steady breath. And I realized—this is what grace feels like. Not erasure. Not perfection. Just the quiet freedom to be here—alive, unarmored. I no longer felt haunted. I felt held.

Letting go doesn't erase the story; it reshapes the way it lives inside you. It turns sorrow into space, pain into possibility. And that grace—the kind that frees without forgetting—isn't just mine.

It waits for all of us. Because grace is the doorway to everything that comes next. It loosened my grip enough to notice presence in places I once overlooked. It reminded me that even in silence, I was never abandoned. And it was grace that prepared me for the hardest lesson of all: what it means to reach for God when He feels impossibly far, and still achingly close.

My story began with a fist. I didn't know how to unclench. I mistook tension for strength and silence for peace. I carried both like armor, afraid of what might surface if I ever let go. Tonight, my hands are open. My breath is steady. My life has made room for grace. I have found grace, but I am still learning how to find God in the quiet that follows. And maybe that's what faith really is—not certainty, but the willingness to listen for love in the stillness.

CHAPTER 23

When God Went Quiet

*The faith that endured even
when the silence felt endless*

THERE HAVE BEEN MOMENTS IN MY LIFE when God felt so far
away, I wasn't sure He was listening at all. Times when grief pressed
heavy on my chest, the silence rang louder than any hymn, and the
pain was too sharp to make sense of anything sacred. I did not stop
believing, but I struggled to find a way to reach Him through the
fog. The truth is that silence was not new to me. I was raised in it.
Our house carried silence around grief, silence around emotions,
silence around tenderness. So when God went quiet, it did not feel
foreign. It echoed the silence I already knew, the silence I had been
shaped by. In a way, God's silence and my family's silence braided
together until I could not tell them apart.

I remember being a little girl sitting in the kitchen while my
grandmother hummed as she stirred pots on the stove. Her humming was low and steady, not for performance but for peace. I didn't
understand the words of the hymn, but I understood the calm it
carried. Across the room my mother passed by, lips pressed thin,
her silence a kind of wall. Between them I learned two languages
of faith: one that sang even when words were scarce, and one that
stayed quiet out of necessity.

There were nights when I whispered prayers into my pillow, prayers too small to ever reach heaven. I prayed for my dad to show up to a basketball game. I prayed for the sound of gunshots outside to stop. I prayed for my mother to laugh the way she used to. When the prayers went unanswered, I decided maybe God was like my father, close enough to name, too far to rely on.

God's silence later in my life felt like an extension of that inheritance. I did not know if it meant He was gone, or if He was simply present in a way I hadn't yet learned to recognize. In those seasons, I didn't need sermons. I needed presence. A God who could sit with me on the bathroom floor while I tried to catch my breath. A God who didn't require the right words or posture, just honesty. Just a heartbeat. Many nights I laid in bed whispering into the dark, Where are You? And still, something deep in me whispered back, Keep going. Maybe that was God. Maybe it was the part of me I had been trying to silence, the part that still hoped for more.

I have been baptized three times. If I am honest, I don't think I fully understood the purpose of any of them. The first time, I was a kid. A childhood friend named Lisa invited me to church with her family one Sunday. A few days before that, she had handed me a small box and said, "Hold this for a second." I thought it was leftovers. It wasn't. It was her father's cremation. Before I could process it, she looked at me and said, "You need to get right with Jesus before you end up in a box too."

Lisa was the kind of friend who talked about Jesus with the same urgency she used when telling me the rapture could happen before lunchtime. And honestly, given the neighborhood we grew up in, her warning didn't feel that far-fetched. That Sunday, I followed her to church. She told me it was time to get saved, and before I could even process what that meant, I was standing in front of a congregation, repeating the words everyone said I should.

I didn't find God that day, just the uneasy weight of someone else's father, but I did find a strange kind of love in her insistence. Her faith was clumsy but sincere, the kind of certainty I both admired and feared. Even then, I think I understood that belief could be loud for some and quiet for others. Mine just hadn't found its voice yet.

That first baptism was more performance than transformation. It seemed simple enough: say the lines, get washed in water, come out new. But inside, I felt the same. My hair was wet, but my heart was untouched. I joke now that after three baptisms I should at least get a free coffee or a T-shirt. But the quieter truth is this: I wanted to believe. I wanted to belong. I just didn't know how to stay.

Faith always carried a tension for me, especially in Black church spaces. On one hand, they felt like home, rich with history, rooted in resilience, pulsing with the strength that carried generations through the impossible. But they could also feel heavy with unspoken rules. Where "Sunday best" wasn't just about clothes, it was about posture. About keeping your voice steady when everything in you wanted to break. Those spaces gave me glimpses of belonging, but they also reminded me of every place I had been asked to perform.

And it wasn't just church. Even at home, I lived between performance and silence. My grandmother hummed hope. My mother carried her faith like a stone in her pocket, present but never spoken of. And I was the one caught in the middle, trying to learn which legacy would become mine. I stayed polite, respectful, engaged enough to look present, but never so vulnerable that anyone could see the cracks. But faith performed eventually runs out of breath. And when the performance faded, all I was left with was silence, God's and my own.

There was a season when God went completely quiet for me. My life looked steady on the outside, career intact, daughter thriving, responsibilities managed, but my spirit felt hollow. I would wake up, put on the uniform, and drive my patrol car through the city with the same precision as always. I responded to calls, comforted families, wrote reports, attended meetings. At home, I cooked dinner, helped Kenzie with homework, and folded laundry. From the outside, nothing looked broken. But inside, I was disappearing.

I remember one call especially. A young boy had been killed in a drive-by. He couldn't have been more than fourteen. He lay on the pavement, sneakers turned awkwardly to the side, a pool of blood spreading beneath him. His mother's scream cut through the night, a sound that seemed to shake the whole block. She dropped to her knees, clutching at him, her body rocking back and forth like she could will him back.

The chaplain's voice rose above her cries, trembling but steady, the words of his prayer breaking against the air like glass. Streetlights hummed. Sirens faded. The smell of gunpowder and hot asphalt hung thick around us. My vest pressed heavy into my shoulders, and sweat clinging to the back of my neck.

I shifted my weight on the curb, hands at my sides, useless. The radio at my hip crackled with static, a voice calling out codes I barely heard. I stared at the boy's face, at the mother's hands gripping him as though she could keep him from slipping away. Everything in me wanted to kneel beside her, to say something, to do anything. But I stood still, swallowed by the enormity of it. Around me, voices prayed, cried, cursed. Inside me, nothing but silence.

At home, the silence followed me. I dropped my bag at the door, forced a smile for Kenzie as she told me about her day, and then collapsed onto the couch after she went to bed. The TV played, the lamp glowed, but I felt like a ghost in my own house. I wasn't praying. I wasn't reaching. I was functioning, not living. That hollowness scared me more than the chaos on the street, because at least there I knew the rules of survival. At home, all I knew was silence.

Looking back, I see He was closer than I realized. In the sisterhood of my sorority. In the women who checked on me when I had no words for my struggle. In the sunlight spilling across my kitchen table when I thought I couldn't keep going. In Kenzie's laughter, her stubborn insistence that I stay present when my mind wanted to drift away. Once, when she was about six, she asked if God could hear her sing. Her voice was small, but the question stopped me cold. I wanted to say yes with certainty. Instead, I told her, "I think He can." Maybe that was for her, but it was also for me.

Those glimpses kept me afloat, but I still longed for something undeniable, something that would break through the walls I had built around my faith. The most unexpected moment came one Sunday, when I decided to try again. I slipped into the back pew of a small church, ready to listen, leave, and check church off my list. The choir began an old hymn I hadn't heard since childhood.

Their voices rose like thunder and honey all at once, and suddenly I was crying. Not polite tears, but the kind that shake your shoulders. My face was hot, my chest heaved, and for a moment I wanted to run. But my feet stayed planted. I closed my eyes and the words of the hymn unlocked a memory, my grandmother's humming in the kitchen, her voice steady over the sound of boiling pots. The hymn was the same one she had sung without words.

And there it was—God impossibly far and achingly close. The weight of all the years I had doubted Him, and the nearness of a love that refused to let me go. That tension, the ache and the comfort, has walked beside me ever since.

Not long after, another small crack appeared in my armor. A woman from church approached me one afternoon and asked if she could pray for me. My first instinct was to decline. I didn't want attention. I didn't want anyone peeking behind the curtain I worked so hard to hold closed. But she placed her hand gently on my shoulder and began anyway, her voice steady, her words ordinary but sincere. Something in me softened. I didn't know if I believed every word she prayed, but I believed the intention. I believed that someone cared enough to stand beside me. That moment did not solve everything, but it reminded me that letting someone hold you up is its own kind of faith.

For a long time, I thought faith was about proving something to God, to others, maybe even to myself. Now I think it is about staying. Even when it's hard. Even when it's quiet. Even when you don't have the answers. Doubt still comes. I used to believe doubt meant failure, that questioning God made my faith weaker. Now I see it differently. Doubt is not the opposite of faith; it is the soil faith grows in. Every question I have asked has pushed me closer to honesty, and honesty is what God has wanted from me all along. Maybe that's what belonging to God has always been about. Not perfection. Not performance. Just coming back.

Faith didn't erase my struggles. But it reshaped how I carried them. It taught me that strength doesn't always look like pushing through or holding everything together. Sometimes it looks like surrender. Sometimes it is quiet. Sometimes it is laying the armor down, trusting you will still be protected.

One morning, after weeks of restless nights, I sat at my kitchen table with a cup of coffee gone cold in my hands. The house was quiet except for the hum of the refrigerator. I closed my eyes, unclenched my jaw, and finally exhaled. It wasn't a polished prayer. It was barely a sentence: I can't carry this alone. Something softened. Not the pain, it was still there, but the grip. In that moment, I let go of the illusion that survival rested only on my shoulders. My body sank into the chair. My shoulders dropped. Sunlight spilled across the table like an answer I hadn't known I was waiting for. Maybe faith was never about me climbing high enough to reach Him—maybe it was about realizing He had been here all along.

Later that day, Kenzie padded into the kitchen, her hair wild from sleep, her pajamas twisted from the night. She climbed into my lap without a word, her small body pressing against mine. She smelled of sleep and warmth, her cheek resting against my chest. She looked up, curious, and asked softly, "Mommy, are you okay?" Her question pierced me more deeply than any sermon could. I swallowed, nodded, and whispered back, "I am now." In her eyes I saw it, the echo of God's presence. The proof that even in silence, I was not alone.

This is the grace I carry forward: my grandmother hummed hymns, my mother shouldered silence, and I, through all my faltering and questioning, am choosing presence. Not the loud kind that demands performance, but the quiet kind that sits in kitchens, pours light across tables, and lets a daughter climb into your lap to ask if you're okay.

Maybe that is faith's truest legacy, not certainty, not doctrine, but presence passed down. My grandmother's whispered songs. My mother's steady hands. And now, Kenzie's laughter rising like a psalm all her own. What I hope she remembers of me is not that I was perfect or unshakable, but that I kept coming back. That faith lived in the way I held her, in the way I chose softness when hardness would have been easier.

Sometimes my prayers are still messy. Not eloquent. Not polished. They sound like laughter spilling through my kitchen, like tears pressed into my daughter's shoulder, like silence finally exhaled after years of holding my breath. But I've learned—they don't have to be perfect to be holy. This is my prayer now: May I keep choosing softness, even when survival calls louder. May I trust that love is not fragile but a birthright. May I remember that home is not a place but a presence—the presence I have finally found within myself.

Because faith didn't just reshape how I reached for God; it reshaped how I understood strength. I thought silence demanded armor. But in the end, it was God's quiet presence that showed me that real strength isn't found in what we hold on to, but in what we finally lay down. I started this journey with God feeling impossibly far away. Now I know He was never distant—only quiet. And even in His silence, I was held. That's the grace of it all: the same stillness that once felt empty became the place I learned to listen, to rest, to return. It's where I began coming home to myself.

CHAPTER 24

Coming Home to Yourself

The peace waiting beneath
every fracture and every scar

THERE WAS A SEASON WHEN my life looked solid on paper. The job. The uniform. A daughter I adored. A house that stood steady. Smiles frozen in picture frames. A calendar stacked with obligations, every hour spoken for. From the outside, I looked like I had it all together. But inside, I was dissolving. Not in flames or spectacle, just a slow erosion. A quiet unraveling no one could see. I was performing strength so well I almost convinced myself it was real.

Until the day I couldn't. It was an ordinary morning. I sat in my car in full uniform, engine humming, radio clipped to my shoulder. I was supposed to walk into work. Instead, I stayed parked. The air was stale with the smell of old coffee I hadn't touched, the leather of the seat pressing into the back of my thighs. My hands gripped the steering wheel so tightly my knuckles turned pale, veins straining against the skin. The weight of my vest pressed into my shoulders, a reminder of the armor I wore on the outside and the armor I couldn't shed inside.

The radio crackled with unfinished sentences, voices calling out codes, the city still moving. A dispatcher's tone was clipped, professional, routine. But nothing in me felt routine. My jaw locked.

My teeth ached from the pressure. My whole body braced as if for impact. My pulse thundered in my ears, each beat like a drum announcing the panic I could no longer hide. My breath came shallow, caught high in my chest. I thought, Just walk inside. Just breathe. Just get through today. But another voice—quieter, sharper—rose up: What if today is the day you can't? What if walking in means disappearing for good?

And then the tears came—violent, unstoppable—the kind born not of sadness but of exhaustion. A soul-deep exhaustion. From carrying. From pretending. From being everything to everyone while quietly abandoning myself. The sobs tore out of me until I could hardly breathe. I pressed my forehead against the steering wheel, the cold surface grounding me as my breath fogged the glass. My body shook as if it was trying to purge years of silence in a single morning. And for the first time, I let it come. No script. No apology. Just the flood of truth I'd been holding back.

That moment wasn't a breakdown—it was a breakthrough. The thin place where the armor finally split and truth began to leak through. And from that opening came a question that refused to leave me: What would it look like to come home to myself? Coming home, I would learn, wasn't about fixing myself; it was about remembering myself. About setting down the tools that once kept me safe but now kept me stuck—the overexplaining, the perfectionism, the constant performing, the fear of softness.

I had mastered survival. I had forgotten how to simply be, so I began again. I cried in front of people. I rested even when the guilt burned in my throat. I stopped apologizing for existing. I set boundaries, and I honored them. I let silence linger where I once rushed to fill it. And in the stillness, I found pieces of myself I thought I had lost. And as I did, I looked back, not with shame, but with compassion. To the little girl who thought love had to be earned. To the young woman who mistook control for safety. To the mother who carried guilt she didn't deserve. I whispered: You did what you had to do to survive. And now, you get to do something different.

One of the ways I began to come home was through writing. I bought a fresh journal—smooth pages, stiff spine—and filled it with words I had never dared to speak. I wrote letters I would never send. Some were apologies without excuses. Others were raw confessions of hurts I had buried so deep I almost forgot they existed. Some were prayers scratched in shaky handwriting. Some were rage, scrawled across the page until the ink bled through. Some were nothing more than ink-stained tears.

The first time I wrote, my hand trembled. My chest tightened as if the paper itself might betray me. But then, something shifted. Each letter became a mirror, reflecting back the pieces of myself I had abandoned: the child told to "fix her face," the young woman who made silence into armor, the mother who hid behind guilt. On the page, I grieved them. And in grieving, I reclaimed them.

One evening, I wrote a letter to my younger self.

Dear little Rashida,

I know you feel unseen. I know you're tired of being told to be quiet, to stop crying, to stay small. I see the way you keep everything inside because you think no one will hold it for you. But you are not too much. Your laugh is not too loud. Your feelings are not a burden. One day, you'll see, your voice is your gift, not your shame.

Another night, my pen drifted to my father.

The Homecoming

Dear Dad,

There were years I convinced myself I didn't need you. That your absence didn't matter. But it did. I wanted you at the games, at the table, in the everyday places where I carried my silence. I don't know if we'll ever be what I once dreamed of, but I need you to know this: I still wanted you. I still do. And forgiving you doesn't erase the ache—it only makes room for something new.

I never mailed it, but the act of writing it broke something loose in me. It reminded me that I could speak tenderness into the parts of myself I had silenced for so long. The letters didn't change the past. They changed me. They became a bridge, teaching me forgiveness, helping me set down burdens I'd carried too long, reminding me that healing isn't about rewriting history. It's about refusing to keep reliving it.

Coming home also meant unbuckling the armor piece by piece—not because I had stopped being strong, but because I was finally safe enough to be soft. I lived like a fortress—impenetrable, self-sufficient, alone. But when the walls finally cracked, light found its way in. Truth poured through the gaps. Grace, too. It was uncomfortable. And holy. I was learning that safety wasn't the absence of threat, but the presence of trust—trust in myself, in love, in the quiet that no longer frightened me.

I think back to those early days in uniform, when strength was scripted and silence was survival. Walking into roll call with my back straight, my face unreadable, my heart hidden so deep even I couldn't reach it. The badge clipped to my chest was supposed to mean protection, but too often it meant invisibility—me becoming whatever the job demanded, even if it cost me myself. Coming home has meant peeling that away, layer by layer. Reminding myself that I am not the badge, not the mask, not the performance. I am more than what I carried.

If I ever seemed cold while you were reaching for me, please know this: it was never about your worth. It was about my wounds. I was surviving with a heart I hadn't yet dared to name. For that silence, for the walls, for the distance: I'm sorry. Not as an excuse, but as an acknowledgment. The work now is presence, not performance. Grace, not guilt. There's a peace that comes when you stop abandoning yourself. A peace I had never known until now.

For Black women, joy is holy. It is protest. It is reclamation. One night, exhausted after a long day, I turned on music in the kitchen. Without thinking, I started to dance. Barefoot, laughing, arms free. For once, I wasn't a mother, officer, or protector. I was just me. Soft. Unburdened. Alive. Later, I sat at the kitchen table, still barefoot, still smiling, and I wrote a letter. Not to anyone else. To me.

Dear Rashida,

I see you. I forgive you. You did what you had to do to make it this far. And now, you don't have to keep fighting the same battles. You don't have to keep proving you're worthy. You are worthy because you are here. You are whole even when you feel broken. You are allowed to rest. You are allowed to be loved. You are allowed to be home in yourself.

I closed the journal, exhaled, and felt the truth settle: coming home isn't one dramatic arrival. It's a quiet return. A slow exhale. A reintroduction to your own voice. Yes, it costs something. You have to grieve the versions of yourself you built for survival. You have to mourn the years you lived silenced, armored, unseen. You have to name the toll that strength-as-performance demanded. But on the other side of that grief is freedom, the kind you feel in your breath, your chest, your unclenched hands.

Sometimes coming home looks ordinary: a deep sigh when the house is quiet. A walk without headphones, letting the wind remind me I have a body, not just a role. Saying no without a list of justifications. Sitting across from someone I trust and telling the truth, even when my voice shakes. Letting myself laugh too loud, eat too slow, cry without apology. Choosing rest instead of working another late shift. Calling someone back not because I had to, but because I wanted to. Laying my head down at night and actually sleeping without bracing for the next alarm. These small acts of honesty, repeated again and again, have stitched me back to myself.

I lived split—daughter and officer, protector and threat, bridge and barrier. I tried to be both, to prove I could belong everywhere. But coming home showed me the truth: I don't have to resolve that tension; I only have to live honestly within it. I am more than those worlds. I am who I am beneath them—soft, steady, and finally at peace. I began this story in silence, taught to hide my tears and carry armor I wasn't allowed to set down. Now I end here, choosing a different inheritance. Choosing to rest without apology. To love without earning. To laugh without bracing. To be soft without shame.

And this isn't just my story. It belongs to anyone who has ever swallowed their voice, who has ever mistaken survival for living, who has ever wondered if they'd lost themselves for good. If that's you, hear me: you can still come home. I was raised to fix my face, to hide my tears, to wear strength like armor. I believed that script was the only way to survive. But I'm not performing anymore. My face is soft now. My tears fall freely. My strength is no longer silence—it is voice, it is rest, it is joy. I think of my great-grandmother—her hands steady from years of labor, her faith carried more in action than in words, reminding me that God can be found in the quiet. I think of my grandmother—back straight, grief unspoken, her softness hidden behind duty. I think of my mother—always composed, her busyness a shield against collapse. And I think of my daughter—unafraid to tell me I can cry, unafraid to giggle barefoot across the kitchen. Four generations, one long story. And here I am, in the middle, choosing to rewrite the ending.

If you are reading this with clenched hands, holding yourself together so tightly you've forgotten how it feels to breathe, this is for you. May you feel your shoulders drop. May you feel your chest rise and fall with ease. May you taste the freedom of a laugh that doesn't brace for loss. May you remember what it feels like to rest without guilt, to be loved without condition, to trust your own voice again.

> *May you find silence that heals, not silence that hides.*
> *May you find strength that softens, not strength that hardens.*
> *May you find joy that resists despair, peace that resists chaos, and*
>   *love that resists fear.*
> *May you honor those who came before you without carrying their*
>   *burdens as your own.*
> *May you forgive yourself for the years you only knew survival.*
> *And may you trust that softness will not break you—it will*
>   *free you.*

Coming home is not a single arrival. It is a rhythm, a practice, a return. Sometimes it looks like silence honored, sometimes like tears welcomed, sometimes like joy spilling into a kitchen with no audience but you. Permission to break was never the end—it was the beginning. The beginning of a life where silence no longer defined me, and softness could finally be my strength. And when the breaking comes—and it will—may you remember this: breaking is not the end. Breaking is where the light pours through. Breaking is where you begin again. This is your invitation. Permission to rest. Permission to be held. Permission to be fully, gloriously human. Welcome home.

I had been surviving for so long that I forgot what it felt like to live. Coming home to myself meant laying down the weight, forgiving the versions of me that only knew how to endure, and choosing softness without apology. Before I close, I want to pause here—for the ones still carrying what feels uncarryable. I hope these pages reminded you that even the heaviest things can be set down, that we are never as alone as silence once made us believe.

The ember still burns—
proof that what remains is light.

Epilogue

The work continues, but so does the beauty

WHAT USED TO ECHO AS ACHE now hums like peace. Sometimes the smallest act—returning to your body, to this moment—is its own form of survival. This is where healing begins: in the quiet decision to stay, to soften, to keep choosing yourself.

The silence that once stayed has softened. For so long, I believed strength meant never breaking. I believed silence was safety. But strength without softness only taught me how to survive. Softness taught me how to live.

Becoming isn't a finish line or a fixed destination. It isn't the last page, the perfect chapter, or the neat bow tied around a story. Becoming is a return—again and again—to the parts of ourselves we buried, the truths we silenced, and the love we thought we had lost. I used to think healing meant being done—that I'd arrive somewhere steady, where the grief no longer stung and the wounds no longer whispered. But the work was never about being unbreakable. It was about granting myself permission to break open and trusting that what rises in the cracks is softer, truer, and more free.

There will be days when silence feels heavy again, when survival creeps back in, convincing you to armor up, when the old voice returns and tells you you're too much. On those days, remember this: healing doesn't mean you'll never ache again. It means you'll know how to meet the ache with gentleness instead of judgment—with presence instead of performance.

Wherever you come from, whoever you are, if you have ever felt unseen, unheard, or unloved, know this: your story matters. Your voice matters. You matter. We were never meant to be stitched together by perfection. We were woven—by God, by breath, by love that cannot be undone. Breaking doesn't separate you from that love; it brings you closer to it.

I don't have all the answers. I am still becoming, still unlearning, still practicing softness. But I know this for sure: you don't have to carry it all to be worthy of love. You don't have to be perfect to begin again. You are allowed to break. That is the permission I gave myself. May it live with you too.

With love and truth, Rashida

Acknowledgments

Gratitude to those who helped carry the load

This book is not mine alone. It was born from the strength, love, and quiet endurance of so many souls who walked with me through the mess, the silence, the breakthroughs, and the beauty of becoming.

To my family: You are my beginning. In ways both seen and unseen, you shaped me. Your resilience etched itself into my bones, teaching me how to survive, how to press forward when it felt impossible, and how to carry on with dignity even when joy felt out of reach. I honor your sacrifices, your strength, and the complexity of our love.

To the friends who became family and the mentors who poured wisdom into me: thank you for showing up. For listening without rushing me. For asking the hard questions and staying through the long silences. For reminding me, gently and sometimes firmly, of who I am, even when I forgot. Your presence was a lifeline.

To my high school English teacher, Ms. White, thank you for seeing my voice before I knew what it could become. You nurtured my love for storytelling and taught me that words could hold power, truth, and beauty all at once. The confidence you sparked in that classroom has followed me ever since, guiding me back to the page every time I lost my way.

Acknowledgments

To the therapists and healers who sat with me in my grief and stood with me in my growth: thank you for helping me gather the pieces. You held space for my tears and my truth, and in doing so, helped me believe that healing was not only possible, but mine to claim.

To my daughter: You are my light, my mirror, my reason. Becoming your mother opened me up in the best way. You taught me how to feel, how to soften, and how to love without armor. Every word in this book holds a piece of that transformation. I pray you always know how deeply you are loved, and that softness is strength.

To the ancestors whose blood runs through mine: thank you. I carry your prayers, your pain, and your perseverance. This book is part of your legacy. Your survival made my healing possible. To every community I have belonged to, passed through, or held in my heart: thank you for your stories, your truths, your pain, and your celebration. Whether rooted in my hometown or scattered across the world, you have taught me what it means to belong, to be broken open, and still be worthy of love.

And to you, the reader, thank you for picking up this book and stepping into my story. Whether you came here out of curiosity, connection, or your own quiet search for healing, I see you. I wrote this with you in mind. May you find something here that mirrors your journey, honors your wounds, and whispers to the strongest parts of you, even if they have gone quiet.

This is more than my story. It is ours, woven with truth, courage, and a deep hope that we can all rise together. From the depths of my soul, thank you.

With love and truth, Rashida

About the Author

The story behind the storyteller

Rashida Saunders was born and raised in Portland, Oregon, and has dedicated over sixteen years to public service, first in juvenile corrections and later as a police officer. She plans to retire in the same uniform she wears today, with honor, grit, and love for her city.

At her core, Rashida is a mother. She calls it the most demanding and beautiful role of her life, one that has shaped the way she leads, protects, and heals. A true daughter of the "Rose City," Rashida is a product of Portland's public and parochial schools, including Martin Luther King Jr. Elementary, Harriet Tubman and Ockley Green Middle School, and De La Salle North Catholic High School. She went on to earn a BA in Criminal Justice and an MA in Justice Administration and Security.

Her career has spanned roles from juvenile detention officer to police officer, Crisis Response Team Coordinator, Juvenile Runaway Officer, and Sunshine Division Liaison, where she helps lead city-wide efforts to fight food insecurity and support families in need. Her dedication has been recognized with numerous commendations and community awards throughout her career, honoring both her professional excellence and her commitment to community care. Whether through organizing "Shop with a Cop" or delivering

208

care directly to families' doorsteps, Rashida shows up with heart, integrity, and humility.

She is also a proud member of Alpha Kappa Alpha Sorority, Inc., the first historically Black sorority, founded on the pillars of sisterhood, scholarship, and service. Her devotion to community reflects the values of her beloved sisterhood.

Rashida is the founder of Black Ember Press, her independent publishing imprint dedicated to amplifying stories of strength, healing, and community. *Permission to Break* is the press's first title and her debut memoir, marking the beginning of her journey as an author and storyteller committed to truth and healing.

Across every role she has held, Rashida is guided by a belief in second chances, the power of community, and the courage of vulnerability. She became a certified life coach, expanding her calling to help others move beyond survival and toward wholeness.

Beyond her service and writing, Rashida is a photographer and creative storyteller, capturing resilience, love, and community through her lens. Her travels across Africa, Europe, and South America continue to shape the way she sees stories, serving as reminders that healing, resilience, and love are universal.

When she is not writing or serving her community, Rashida is traveling the world or laughing at home with her daughter, the place she finds her greatest joy. She also speaks on healing, leadership, and community resilience.

Guided by faith, Rashida hopes her work reminds others that softness is not weakness, that healing is among the bravest acts of all, and that true legacy is measured not only in strength but in the tenderness we pass on to the next generation.

About Black Ember Press

Why this imprint was born and what it stands for

This imprint was born from fire, the kind that doesn't destroy but transforms. The kind that smolders in silence until it finally breaks into light. Black Ember Press was created for the stories we were once too afraid to tell. For the voices overlooked. For the truths that made people uncomfortable. For the Black girls told to be quiet. For the women who survived by hardening. For anyone who has carried silence and still dared to speak.

We exist because sometimes you have to build the table when you're not offered a seat. Because representation should never be rare. Because healing deserves a home. The ember in our name is a reminder that even after the flames fade, something powerful still burns. From that glow, stories rise. Black Ember Press is a space for rawness, reckoning, and reclamation, for grief and joy in the same breath. Here, truth is honored, and softness is not weakness. It is revolution—not the kind that burns everything down, but the kind that rebuilds us from within.

Resources

For the moments when the weight feels
too heavy to carry alone

Here you'll find places of refuge, support, and guidance, reminders that you were never meant to walk this path by yourself. If you are struggling, know this: you are not alone. Reaching for support is not weakness. It is strength.

In the United States
- 988 Suicide & Crisis Lifeline—Dial or text 988 anytime to connect with trained crisis counselors, 24/7.
- Crisis Text Line—Text HOME to 741741 to connect with a counselor by text message.
- National Domestic Violence Hotline—Call 1-800-799-SAFE (7233) or text START to 88788 for confidential support.
- SAMHSA Helpline—Call 1-800-662-HELP (4357) for treatment referrals and information on mental health and substance use.

Outside the United States
- Visit findahelpline.com, which lists hotlines worldwide.
- Or search for crisis and suicide prevention hotlines in your country.

Other Supports

- Reach out to a trusted friend, family member, therapist, or spiritual leader.
- Journaling, grounding practices, and community support groups can also provide care while you seek help.

You deserve help.
You deserve healing.
You deserve to stay.

Grounding Practice

A gentle way to return to yourself

Take one deep breath in, and let it out slowly.
Notice three things you can see around you.
Notice two things you can touch near you.
Notice one sound you can hear.

You are here.
You are safe in this moment.
You are not alone.